Dean Posey's book, *12 Gifts We Can't Afford to Lose* is a must read for every church planter and seasoned pastor. Every Christian leader will greatly benefit from Pastor Posey's insights and applications for years to come. Be sure to read it and get extra copies for your peers!

Michael Knight
Founder, Global Coaching Network
National Church Planting, Church of God

In *12 Gifts We Can't Afford to Lose*, Pastor Dean Posey teaches us how to navigate successfully through the storms that come our way. There can be no doubt that this generation is living in unparalleled times and will face some of the most significant challenges of any era. Old maps will not work in new territories. Be sure to purchase your copy of *12 Gifts We Can't Afford to Lose* today!

Elmer L. Towns
Liberty University, Cofounder

12 Gifts We Can't Afford to Lose empowers Christians everywhere to be prepared for the storms coming to this generation. Pastor Dean Posey has brought together his decades of pastoral ministry and collective wisdom in his book. In tumultuous times, his powerful resource will help you to sail through the storms of life and make it to the other side!

Dr, John Ed Mathison
Frazier Memorial United Methodist Church, Pastor Emeritus
John Ed Mathison Leadership Ministries, Founder/President

Storms are inevitable! Growth is optional! Dean Posey's book, *12 Gifts We Can't Afford to Lose* Lose will equip you and your team to survive, strive and succeed through life's greatest challenges, coming your way in the future. Read it today and reap for years to come!

Dr. James O. Davis
Co⌐
Founa

D1515887

Rev. Dean Posey's book, *12 Gifts We Can't Afford to Lose* is just the answer to help prepare us to survive the futuristic storms approaching this generation. You will find this dynamic resource to be both principled and practical, addressing all major areas of your life. I encourage you to secure a box of this book for you and your entire team.

Dr. Doug Beacham
Presiding Bishop
International Pentecostal Holiness Church

Dr. Posey has a keen ability of transforming this ancient story into examples and stories relevant to today. *12 Gifts We Can't Afford to Lose* is an easy read full of powerful life-changing lessons.

Bill Bowie
Owner, Olenjack's Grille

12 Gifts We Can't Afford to Lose is a great reminder of the many blessings we have available to us on a daily base. They are well within our reach. Dr. Posey's message gently reminds us that we make a conscious choice each day to accept the gifts from God, or not.

Brent Pilgrim
Director of Services, Beck Technology
Dallas, Texas

12

GIFTS
WE CAN'T
AFFORD
TO LOSE

12 GIFTS
WE CAN'T
AFFORD
TO LOSE

What Noah can teach us about Surviving the Storms of Life and Living Well

DR. DEAN POSEY

BILLIONSOUL
PUBLISHING®

Oviedo, Florida

12 Gifts We Can't Afford to Lose—What Noah Can Teach Us about Surviving the Storms of Life and Living Well
By Dean Posey

Published by Billion Soul Publishing
400 Fontana Circle Building 1, Suite 105
Oviedo, Florida 32765
(407) 563-4806
www.billionsoulpub.com

Unless otherwise indicated all Scripture references are taken from the HOLY BIBLE, NEW INTERNATIONAL VERSION®. Copyright © 1973, 1978, 1984 by International Bible Society. Used by permission of Zondervan Publishing House.

The "NIV" and "New International Version" trademarks are registered in the United States Patent and Trademark Office by International Bible Society. Use of either trademark requires the permission of the International Bible Society.

Scriptures marked NRSV are taken from the New Revised Standard Version of the Bible, copyright 1989, Division of Christian Education of the National Council of the Churches of Christ in the United States of America. Used by permission. All rights reserved.

ISBN: 978-0-9907578-0-1 paperback
ISBN: 978-1-939183-62-0 hardback

Printed in the United States of America.

14 15 16 17 – 9 8 7 6 5 4 3 2 1
Printed in the United States of America

To Sunshine

My soul mate, best friend and wife.

Your smile is contagious, your heart is overflowing, and your spirit is radiant.

It is a humble privilege to share this life with you.

Table of Contents

Acknowledgements

The genesis of the material for this book came over twenty years ago during a quiet time of personal meditation and prayer. However, in order to develop these thoughts and bring them to maturity, many people have been involved. The list of people who have helped along the way is extensive, but there are a few who have assisted at crucial times and in specific ways.

First, my wife Diana, who I call "Sunshine" has listened, guided and been my sounding board from the beginning.

My spiritual mentors and friends, Troy Clinesmith and Richard Freeman, helped mold my life and my faith and have been remarkable role models and mentors.

Karen Searfoss typed my initial hand-written hieroglyphics into readable type.

My previous congregations smiled and stayed awake as I taught and fine-tuned these lessons.

My father and mother in-law, Gene and Pat Coe, were some of the first people to read the rough manuscript and have encouraged me during this entire journey.

Our daughter, Trisha, was my first editor and a great cheerleader. She realized as she read the manuscript, that just like I had talked about and embarrassed her and our son their whole lives from the pulpit, I was doing the same thing again in print.

Our son Matt and daughter-in-love Gracie continuously boosted my spirits with their loving inquiries about my progress on the book.

I want to say thank you to the members of Trinity United Methodist Church for their support, encouragement and prayers and for their help in choosing the book cover. I am privileged to work with an amazing staff at Trinity who have been very positive and caring. It is a joy to go to work every day. Within Trinity, there is a very special group of people called appropriately, "The Noah Committee." Knowing that all the funds generated from the sale of this book will help the Arlington community through the development of the Trinity Sports Ministry, the Noah Committee has generously donated hours of their time to this cause.

Most of all, I want to thank Bill and Shari Bowie who caught the vision for the book and the Trinity Sports Ministry and supported this dream. Without them, this book would never have been published.

To all of these and many more—you are gifts that I can't afford to lose.

Introduction

Are We Willing to Receive?

Jackie's mother died just before his ninth birthday. After that he lived with his father on their farm.

With only one parent in the household, life can be difficult. That's how it was for Jackie because he had to do most of the household chores and meal preparation while his father worked in the fields. On school days, their morning ritual was always the same. Jackie and his father got up before dawn to begin their chores. Jackie cooked breakfast. While he washed the dishes, his father went out to start the old pickup. The truck never started the first time, or even the third or fourth time. However, when it did finally start, his father backed up to the front door, and Jackie would run and jump into the truck.

This ritual happened every day, rain or shine. On one of those cold, wet days, instead of looking at the floorboard or out the window, Jackie looked at his father. He noticed the lines in his face that had been carved by the bitter wind. He saw his broad shoulders and his muscular arms. Jackie noticed his father's hands. He could see calluses and bruises through the holes in his gloves. The moment he saw those hands, he instantly knew what he was going to buy his father for his birthday in six weeks.

After school that day, he talked to his teacher about helping at the school to make some money so he could buy his father a present. The teacher agreed to pay Jackie twenty-five cents a day ($1.25 each week), which meant it would take five weeks for him to save enough money to buy a new pair of gloves. Jackie was so excited.

Even though he had to stay up a little later at night to finish his chores at home, the five weeks went by quickly.

The day finally came when Jackie had enough money. His teacher went with him to buy the new gloves. His father's birthday was a few days later, and Jackie was full of anticipation. Their morning ritual was just the same as always, but the moment Jackie jumped into the truck, he looked at his father and said, "Dad, just a minute, I have a birthday present for you." He carefully unzipped his heavy coat and pulled out a brown paper bag that had been squeezed tightly at the top. His father opened the sack, took out the gloves, looked at them for a second and said, "Oh, new gloves," and then threw the gloves behind the seat. Jackie could barely keep from crying. He had worked and sacrificed to give a gift from a heart of love, and all his father could do was toss the gift behind the seat.

I wonder how often we are just like Jackie's father—recipients of beautiful gifts from a heart of love. Without realizing it, we have taken those gifts God gave us and tossed them behind the seat of our lives.

In this book, I focus upon twelve specific gifts that you and I have been offered from the heart of a faithful Heavenly Father. I believe all twelve gifts are described within the story of Noah and the ark. Each chapter of this book focuses upon a different part of this same story. We could get caught up in wondering whether the story of Noah and the ark really happened. We could ask, "Is it historically correct?" However, instead of focusing attention on historical questions, I want to focus attention upon religious questions such as: What does this story teach us about God's faithfulness and His interaction with human life? As we look at this story, we see a loving God who is willing and able to give incredible gifts to humankind.

How can we gratefully receive the gifts God offers? How can we embrace and apply these gifts so that our lives will be better for it? What hinders us from doing so? If the story of Noah and the ark teaches us about our Heavenly Father's faithfulness, how can we apply these lessons to our daily lives?

It is my belief that these twelve gifts are proof that we have been blessed by God's faithfulness and are gifts we can't afford to lose.

Questions

■ How do you wish Jackie's father had responded? What are your initial thoughts about the story of Noah and the ark?

■ What thoughts come to your mind as you consider this book's title?

1

Gift One

The Word

So God said to Noah…

—Genesis 6:13

y wife, Diana, and I went on a trip to Europe. We had wanted to go on that trip for a long time, and we started planning for it a year before we left. After we decided when and where to go, I took responsibility to find hotels while Diana researched what we would do in each city. The first city we stopped in was Brussels, Belgium. Wow! What an amazing place.

I wanted to find a hotel near the center of town because there were so many things to do there. I found a hotel and made a reservation, and then I discovered that, according to my best guess, there were eight chocolate stores within two blocks of the hotel. When we actually got to Brussels, I discovered that I was totally wrong. There were more than twenty chocolate shops within that distance, including the original Godiva chocolate store. Right across the street from our hotel was a place called The Chocolate Planet. It was wonderful! There were so many choices.

A few days later we were in the city of Delft, in the Netherlands. Every morning at breakfast we had the opportunity to make a choice. After you toasted your bread and spread Nutella on it, you could make another choice. You could then put dark or light chocolate on your Nutella: shaved or sprinkles. So many choices—so many good choices!

Life is full of choices, isn't it? I believe the most important life choice is choosing to believe in Jesus Christ as our Lord and Savior. Jesus died on the cross so we could have forgiveness of our sins. He rose from the dead so we could have the gift of eternal life. When we accept Him as our Lord and Savior, He literally changes our life. There is no other choice that comes close to the importance of choosing Jesus as our Lord and Savior.

Some other important choices in life are:

- Will we get married and to whom?
- How do we find satisfaction and fulfillment in life?
- What do we do about a career?
- What do we believe about the Bible?

The first gift from God we can't afford to lose is the gift of God's Word. As we think about the Word of God, there are at least three reasons why His Word is a gift.

First, the Word of God is a gift because it is through the Word of God that we discover the heart of God.

I believe the Bible is the inspired, authentic, trustworthy, truthful, without error Word of God. It's not just a book about God. It's not just a book that contains the truth. No, it is the Word of God and is the Truth! The questions about the Bible and our lives are many. Some examples include the following:

- Are we going to live life according to the truth of the Word of God?

- Is the Bible going to be our final authority in life?

- When life does not line up with the Word of God, do we change so that our character lines up with the Word of God?

- Or do we live the way we want and then discount the Word of God, and say that part of the Word does not apply?

The one choice about the authority of the Word of God in life affects so many other life choices.

In Genesis 6, we read about an amazing man named Noah. The Bible says in Genesis 6:9, *"Noah was a righteous man...and he walked with God."* Wow! What an amazing life he must have lived.

Next, let's read Genesis 6:11–12, *"Now the earth was corrupt.... [A]ll the people on earth had corrupted their ways."* There was sinfulness, corruption, ungodliness, and unholiness. However, in the midst of all that, there was Noah—a righteous and godly man. I see a lot of similarities between the world in Noah's time and today, but I am writing to encourage you to know that it is still possible to live a godly, holy, and righteous life before God and people. It depends upon how much authority we give the Word of God in our lives.

One of the main reasons Noah was righteous and godly was that he was willing to listen and be obedient to the Word of God. In Genesis 6:13, we read, *"So God said to Noah."* The word "said" is the same word that is used in Genesis 1:3, when we read, *"And God said, 'Let there be light,' and there was light."* When God speaks:

- Universes form out of nothing
- Chaos turns into order
- Where once there was nothing—now there is something

Can you imagine what was happening in the heart of God at the time of Noah? His creativity and His created order were turned back into chaos. However, in the midst of all that, Noah was the one man who still chose to connect to and rely upon God. So God spoke once again. When He spoke to Noah, God shared His heart and His purpose. In the coming chapters, we look deep into this story of Noah and discover that when God spoke to Noah, it was not primarily about destruction. Rather, it was primarily about salvation. Let's not miss that truth or reverse it. God had a plan. His plan was to bring salvation.

Today, God continues to speak to humankind through His Word. Today, He still speaks for salvation, not for destruction, as can be seen in the following Scriptures:

- John 3:16: *"For God so loved the world that He gave His one and only Son that whoever believes in Him shall not perish but have eternal life."*

- 2 Peter 3:9: *"The Lord is not slow in keeping His promise, as some understand slowness. He is patient with you, not wanting anyone to perish, but everyone to come to repentance."*

God's heart desires that everyone know Jesus as their Lord and Savior. It is one of the main reasons God continues to speak through His Word. I truly believe that when we listen to and are obedient to the Word of God, as was Noah, then God can work in us and through us to bring the salvation of Jesus Christ into the chaos of a sinful and dying world.

Second, the Word of God is a gift because it is through the Word of God that we discover the desires of God.

Our salvation in Jesus Christ is not the end of God's purposes for His Word in our lives. Rather it is just the beginning. After we choose to have faith in Christ, God's desire is for us to grow in our faith. His desire is for us to grow in godliness, to grow in holiness, and to continue growing until we, like Noah, walk with God.

In 2 Timothy 3:16–17, we read, *"All Scripture is God-breathed and is useful for teaching, rebuking, correcting, and training in righteousness, so that the man of God may be thoroughly equipped for every good work."* What the apostle Paul was saying to Timothy, and to us, is that the Word of God—the God-breathed truth of God— can guide us, direct us, and teach us the ways of God.

We do not just believe in Jesus as our Lord and Savior, but we also choose to align our lives with the Word of God so that we grow in godliness, grow in righteousness, and grow in holiness.

The world today is in much the same chaos that the world was in during the time of Noah. I believe that God is speaking out to you and me—inviting us and also challenging us to be a people of His book. It is His desire for us to be a people who choose to live and grow according to His ways and His truth.

Third, the Word of God is a gift because it is through the Word of God that we discover the power of God.

Have you ever seen a set of architectural drawings for a building? Many decisions go into constructing a building of any size. What if you had plans and they looked good, but a decision was made to not follow them for the electrical system, the plumbing system, or the air-conditioning system? You would have a building, but the quality would be inferior. Problems would be massive and frustrations would be high.

The outcome is obvious when we ask those questions with architectural drawings that just involve a building. Now imagine what would happen if we did the same thing with our life and the Bible? God is the master architect of life. He is also the master architect of godliness and holiness. When we choose to align our life with His truth, it is amazing the joy and peace we experience in daily living. However, when our priorities, motives, or actions vary from the Truth of the Word of God, the result is sadness, emptiness, and chaos—as it was in the days of Noah.

Two purposes of the Word of God are:

1. To help us discover the heart of God which is to bring all people to faith in Jesus Christ

2. To help us discover the desire of God which is for us to grow in faith and godliness

Another purpose of the Word of God is to help us realize that we cannot live a holy and godly life by our own strength and power:

> *For our struggle is not against flesh and blood, but against the rulers, against the authorities, against the powers of this dark world and against the spiritual forces of evil in the heavenly realms. Therefore put on the full armor of God, so that when the day of evil comes, you may be able to stand your ground, and after you have done everything, to stand. Stand firm then, with the belt of truth buckled around your waist, with the breastplate of righteousness in place, and with your feet fitted with the readiness that comes from the gospel of peace. In addition to all this, take up the shield of faith, with which you can extinguish all the flaming arrows of the evil one. Take the helmet of salvation and the sword of the Spirit, which is the word of God (Ephesians 6:12–17).*

We are in a battle and the enemy is more powerful than we realize, but the One whose book is THE BOOK is greater and more powerful than all the enemies we will ever face. When we and others face the enemy of:

- Sin—the Word of God tells us that we are forgiven in Jesus

- Guilt and shame—the Word of God tells us that we can be set free in Jesus

- Hopelessness—the Word of God brings the hope of Jesus

- Loneliness—the Word of God assures us of the presence of Jesus

- Anger and resentment—the Word of God brings the power of the love of Jesus

- Whatever adversary you and I face—the person we can count on to fight those battles is Jesus, and the weapon He always uses is the Word of God

One of the most important decisions we will ever make in life is about how much authority we will give the Word of God. For you, is the Bible simply a book about God? Or is it the Word of God—a book that is authentic, trustworthy, and truthful? For me, the Bible is the Word of God. My desire is to live my life following Jesus and be a man of One Book. Today, the world needs a people of One Book who are dedicated to living according to the Word of God. Let us be those people. Let us be so bold as to live our lives according to the truth of God and hear God's voice as did Noah, so He can use your life and mine to bring the salvation of Jesus to a hurting world. It is one of the most important choices you and I will ever make.

Questions

- What would you add to the list of important life decisions?

- Summarize your view of God's Word.

- How does the Bible help us discover God?

- What questions would you ask Noah if you could talk to him now?

2

Gift Two
Faith

The LORD saw how great man's wickedness on the earth had become, and that every inclination of the thoughts of his heart was only evil all the time. The LORD was grieved that he had made man on the earth, and his heart was filled with pain. So the LORD said, "I will wipe mankind, whom I have created, from the face of the earth—men and animals, and creatures that move along the ground, and birds of the air— for I am grieved that I have made them." But Noah found favor in the eyes of the LORD.

This is the account of Noah.

Noah was a righteous man, blameless among the people of his time, and he walked with God. Noah had three sons: Shem, Ham and Japheth.

Now the earth was corrupt in God's sight and was full of violence. God saw how corrupt the earth had become, for all the people on earth had corrupted their ways. So God said to Noah, "I am going to put an end to all people, for the earth is filled with violence because of them. I am surely going to destroy both them and the earth. So make yourself an ark of cypress wood; make rooms in it and coat it with pitch inside and out. This is how you are to build it: The ark is to be 450 feet long, 75 feet wide and 45 feet high. Make a roof for it and finish the ark to within 18 inches of the top. Put a door in the side of the ark and make lower, middle and upper decks. I am going to bring floodwaters on the earth to destroy all life under the heavens, every creature that has the breath of life in it. Everything on earth will perish. But I will establish my covenant with you, and you will enter the ark—you and your sons and your wife and your sons' wives with you. You are to bring into the ark two of all living creatures, male and female, to keep them alive with you. Two of every kind of bird, of every kind of animal and of every kind of creature that moves along the ground will come to you to be kept alive. You are to take every kind of food that is to be eaten and store it away as food for you and for them."

Noah did everything just as God commanded him.

—Genesis 6:5–22

The second gift from God we can't afford to lose is the gift of faith. To talk about this gift of faith, I want to focus upon the first part of the story about Noah and the ark. The first part begins in Genesis 6:5 and continues through Genesis 6:22. God looked out upon the earth and saw that the earth was filled with human violence and corruption. He made a decision to destroy the entire human population except for one family. That one family was the family of Noah, a man who God had looked upon with favor. God told Noah that He wanted Noah to build an ark, and He told him how big the ark was to be. Then God told Noah why he was doing this. There was to be a flood of such gigantic proportion that it would destroy all human life except his family. The flood would also destroy all animal life, except the animals that would be in the ark.

This story teaches us that one gift that comes from God is the gift of faith. Through this story of Noah we discover four reasons why faith is a gift we can't afford to lose.

First, faith is a gift because it is through faith that we begin a relationship with God through His Son, Jesus Christ.

Several months ago I drove by a barbeque restaurant, as I had many times, and noticed a new sign out front that read, "Under New Management." That is exactly what happens when we turn our lives over to Jesus and begin a relationship with God through His Son. We are putting out a sign saying "Under New Management." We are not allowing ourselves to be managed by ourselves any longer. We are transferring our trust and putting ourselves under the management of Jesus so we can follow His directions for our lives.

There are many benefits of the new management. One is the free gift of heaven. Another is the immediate forgiveness of our sins. That Jesus forgives sin is one of the greatest truths of the Bible—period. We no longer have to carry the garbage, baggage, and junk that happens. We can turn it over to a new Manager, ask forgiveness, and walk away. This does not give us a license to sin, but forgiveness helps us experience every day as a fresh new day with Jesus.

Walking with God is not natural for us. What is natural for us is to think and walk in ungodly ways (Genesis 6:5). God gives us the gift of faith and it comes into our life like a seed. It is up to us to nurture that seed and help it grow. I have a personal responsibility for my own faith. I also have a corporate responsibility to help your faith grow. You have a personal responsibility for your personal faith, but you also have a corporate responsibility to help my faith grow and other people's faith grow. Life is a journey, and one of the opportunities we have along this journey is to make decisions that will help our faith grow and help other people's faith grow as well. In order for our faith to grow, however, we need to be open to being influenced by Jesus Christ.

That brings me to the next reason why faith is so important.

Second, faith is a gift because it is through our faith that we receive God's vision for our life.

First we have a relationship with God, and then He gives us a vision for our life. That order is important even though many people try to make it work the opposite way.

In my opinion, some of the greatest movies of all time are the six *Star Wars* movies. In the last movie, Luke Skywalker becomes a Jedi

Knight. There is a very significant line at the end of the movie when Luke meets the Emperor of Darkness, and the Emperor wants Luke to become the successor to Luke's father. It may be one of the most important lines of all six movies. Luke is about to be killed because he does not want to give himself over to the evil power. Just before the Emperor is to kill him, the Emperor says these words, "You will now pay the consequences for your lack of vision."

That line is not just true in the movies; it is also true in life. One of these days we will pay the consequences, either for our faith that allowed us to accept God's vision or for our lack of faith to accept God's vision.

Do you ever wonder what God's vision is for your life? Sometimes we refer to this as God's will for our life. In 1 Thessalonians 5:16–18 we read, *"Be joyful always; pray continually; give thanks in all circumstances, for this is God's will for you in Christ Jesus."* As we learn to walk with God, this Scripture will become more and more true in our life.

As we begin walking with God, we often realize that God has something specific for us to do. God is active in the world and invites us to join Him in His activity. First we have a relationship with God, and then He gives us a vision for our life. Noah did not come up with the idea of the flood and the ark, and then ask God to bless it. Noah had a relationship with God. As a result of that relationship, Noah heard what God had on His agenda. After hearing what was on God's heart, Noah adjusted his life to participate in God's agenda.

The order of this story is important. First, God developed a relationship with Noah, and then God shared the vision. God always develops a relationship to match the vision. Sometimes, God gives us a vision that will develop our relationship with Him. Other times, He gives us a vision because of that relationship.

A good example of this dynamic is found in the parable of the talents (Matthew 25:14–30). In this parable, the master goes on a journey. Before he leaves, he entrusts his money to three servants. On his return, he asks the servants to tell what they had done with the money. Two of the servants used the money to make more, while one servant hid the money in the ground. The master is pleased with the two servants and angry with the one.

Most people only realize the secondary lesson from this story. This lesson states that the master gives the servants the money to see what they will do with it in his absence. It is a good lesson, with many applications, but it is still secondary because it focuses upon activity. The primary lesson is deeper and focuses upon relationships. The primary lesson is that the master gives the servants the money, not to see what the servants will do with it, but to see what the money will do to the servants. It is the responsibility that reveals the truth about the relationships.

So it was with Noah. Noah had developed a relationship with God (Genesis 6:9, *"he walked with God"*). Then God gave Noah a vision to reveal the depth of that relationship.

The same dynamic happens in your life and mine. God has a desire to develop a deep relationship with us. He will give us a vision to either further develop that relationship or reveal the relationship that is already present. Sometimes we want a larger vision, but we do not yet have the relationship, discipline, or obedience needed to go along with it. As with the parable in Matthew, if we are faithful in the little things, then God will give us a larger vision.

By now you might be asking a great question: how does God reveal His vision for our life? To me, it is like a seed planted in our hearts that needs to be carefully nurtured until the timing is right for it to become public.

For our twenty-fifth anniversary, I built a greenhouse for my wife, Diana. She is passionate about plants, and I wanted to do something unique for our anniversary. She was in Mexico for two weeks with our daughter, Trisha, when the majority of the green-house was built. My wife did not know it was happening. In fact, she was not aware of all the planning that happened at night while she was asleep. Nor was she aware of the materials I purchased and hid at a friend's home prior to her departure to Mexico.

Construction started the day Diana and Trisha left for Mexico. With the help of many friends, the project was almost complete when she returned. Needless to say, my wife was shocked and speechless when our son, Matt, brought her home from the airport. A short time later, the greenhouse was complete and fully opera-tional, and within weeks it was beaming with life and color. Within a year it seemed as if our whole house and yard had been affected by plants or flowers that had spent at least some time in the greenhouse.

Faith can be described in many ways. One of the ways I visu-alize faith is to view it like a greenhouse. It is an environment in our hearts where God can plant His vision for our life. At first, His vision for us is like a seed that needs a safe place to be planted. As that vision begins to grow in our lives, it needs protection from the heat and cold. Many times, visions are removed from the greenhouse too quickly and soon die because of the heat of criticism or the coldness of apathy.

However, there will be a time when the vision is well-rooted and the timing is right. (Some plants cannot survive even one day outside the greenhouse at the wrong time of the year.) It is at that time when we bring God's vision out of the greenhouse and act upon it publicly and let it affect our whole life. The vision that God gave Noah was not just a vision for his life alone. God wanted to also bless future generations through the vision He planted in Noah's heart.

In Genesis 6:14, God planted the seed of vision for the ark in Noah's life. What the story does not tell us is how long Noah prayed about and nurtured that vision before he brought it out of the greenhouse in his heart and began to act upon it publicly. We do not know how long it was before this vision consumed his life and the life of his family. However, Noah knew that once this vision became public, there was no turning back. His obedience to the vision would be crucial.

Let your obedience begin while the vision is still in the greenhouse. That is a time for prayer, planning, and research.

Third, faith is a gift because faith is the foundation for our obedience.

Once we know what God's vision is for our life, the next crucial element is obedience to that vision. Sometimes we do not have a specific plan of action as we begin our obedience.

Beginning too soon without a plan can lead to inactivity and discouragement. However, waiting to begin until every detail has been thoroughly worked out can also often lead to inactivity because there is always more planning to be done. The best solution is a compromise between the two extremes. Let your obedience begin while the vision is still in the greenhouse. That is a time for prayer, planning, and research.

Before the actual construction began on Diana's greenhouse, I did as much research as I knew how to do. I talked to a carpenter and people at two greenhouse manufacturer and supply companies, and read several books and articles on the Internet. The carpenter turned my rough sketches into working drawings. The greenhouse supply companies helped me understand the issues related to windows, ventilators, roofing, shading, heating, and cooling. Before one board was purchased or one hole was dug for the foundation, I knew most of the materials I would need for the project. The day I ordered the polycarbonate for the roof and purchased the windows and lumber was the day when there was no turning back.

Being obedient is simply acting out, day by day, our belief in God's vision for our lives.

Some days I would run out of screws, caulking, or some other type of supplies. This did not stop me from working. I simply worked on another part of the project until I went to the hardware store and bought what I needed.

Before we begin to publicly act on God's vision, we cannot think of everything. We can, however, research and plan many aspects of the vision. As our obedience begins to become public, it is important to use discernment so we can know what activity will add to the accomplishment of the vision and what activity will not.

After God gave Noah the vision of building an ark, Noah was obedient to that vision. We do not know how long this vision was in the planning stage. However, it is important to realize that the planning stage was part of Noah's obedience. Were there any drawings for the ark? How long did those take? How long did it take to obtain all the lumber? Where did he store it before they used it? How much pitch would they need to coat the ark? We do not know the answers to these and many other questions. But the day finally came when Noah's vision became public and, thankfully for all of us, Noah did not turn back.

Yes, he probably received criticism from his neighbors. Yes, people did not understand. Yes, it was hard work. Yes, it took a long time for his obedience to finally reflect God's vision in his life. However, being obedient is simply acting out, day by day, our belief in God's vision for our lives. Many months ago, Diana and I were thinking about buying a bicycle built for two called a tandem. Once I located a used tandem on sale, Diana and I went over to inspect and ride it. When I went to look at the tandem, I met the owner, a forty-eight-year-old man named Paul Smith. We rode the tandem

His whole lifestyle changed because that vision became so important to him.

around his neighborhood so we could get the feel of riding the bicycle. I had never ridden a tandem before, and as we rode around I asked him why he was selling this bicycle. He said he and his wife, Carolyn, began cycling four years earlier and they enjoyed it so much that they kept riding more and more. Finally they wanted to race in a tandem race. They went out and spent $4,000 on a racing tandem bicycle. In fact, they bought two $4,000 bicycles, one for him to be in the front and one for her to be in the front. He told me that their goal was to race in the Race Across America. They wanted to be the first couple over fifty years of age to complete the Race Across America on a tandem bicycle. It had been attempted but had never been completed by a couple over fifty years of age. That became his vision. When that vision gripped his soul, his whole life-style changed because that vision became so important to him. His time commitments changed, his priorities changed, even his financial priorities changed. In fact, every night when he and his wife got home from work, they went out and rode their bicycle for two to three hours.

I wonder how many of us have a vision from God that grips our soul as much as Paul and Carolyn Smith's vision gripped their souls. I wonder how many of us in the church are that obedient to God's vision in our lives. How many of us have allowed God's vision to totally change our lifestyle? How many of us have allowed our obedience to God's vision to change our time commitments, our priorities, and our financial obligations?

How many of us know that what we are doing on a daily basis is being obedient to God's vision for our life?

Do we have a vision from God that is so big and life-changing that when we live in obedience to God, many people's lives are affected in a positive way?

The joy and fulfillment we experience in life is directly proportional to our obedience to God's vision. That means the more obedient we are to God's vision, the more joy and fulfillment we experience in life. In addition, many times the vision God gives us for our lives will not only bring us purpose and fulfillment and joy, but it will also bring blessing and joy to the lives of others. How many of us know that what we are doing on a daily basis is being obedient to God's vision for our life?

In 1975–76, Indiana University's basketball team was undefeated throughout the regular season and captured the NCAA National Championship. Bobby Knight, their controversial coach, led them to that championship. Shortly afterwards, Coach Knight was interviewed on the television show *60 Minutes*. The commentator asked him, "Why is it, Bobby, that your basketball teams in Indiana are always so successful? Is it the will to succeed?" "The will to succeed is important," replied Knight, "but I'll tell you what's more important; it's the will to prepare. It's the will to go out there every day training and building those muscles and sharpening those skills."

That's not just true about basketball. That's also true about life. It was true in the life of Noah and it's also true in your life and mine. Being obedient to the vision of God in our life is something that we should be doing on a daily basis. A friend of mine has a niece named Melissa who was a missionary in Cyprus for two years. At the end of the two years, she wrote me a letter and told me about some of her experiences. She wrote,

> There are three things that I said I would never do: be a teacher, a missionary, or go to seminary! Not only have I learned to never say 'never,' but I have experienced enough to see God's sovereignty work with my obedience. I'm learning that when we walk in obedience, even

when it doesn't make sense, that one step does lead to the next in God's scheme of things. Taking the step is the tough part. It demands that our faith and obedience be released together, even if the step seems outrageous. I hope these steps of faith for me are the foundation for a journey upward that won't end until I reach heaven.

Let's look again at Genesis 6:13–17. In verse 13, God told Noah that the earth was filled with violence. In verse 14, He told Noah that He wanted him to build an ark. In verses 15 and 16, God told him how large the ark was to be. Then in verse 17, God told Noah why he should build an ark. First, God told Noah *what* he was to do and then He told him *why* he was to do it. In your life and mine, many times the same thing happens. First, God tells us what to do and then He tells us why. For Noah, the wait between the what and the why was very short. Some of us are not that fortunate. Sometimes the wait between the what and the why can be very lengthy, and the why comes months or years later. Sometimes God never tells us why.

During those in-between times, the time in-between when God tells us what to do and when He tells us why, our faith and our obedience need to be the strongest. It is in that in-between time that the gift of faith helps us rely upon God. When we are in the gap between the what and the why, being obedient to the vision of God will not only affect our lives, it will also affect the lives of other people. The question we need to ask ourselves is this: are we going to be obedient to what God wants us to do without knowing why?

If our obedience is dependent upon knowing why, that is not obedience; rather, it is arrogance.

Fourth, faith is a gift because faith is the foundation for our salvation.

The cross of Jesus Christ is the foundation for our salvation, but faith is how we accept the salvation that Jesus Christ offers. Genesis 6:15 says the length of the ark shall be 300 cubits, its width 60 cubits, and its height 30 cubits. A cubit was about 18 inches, so that makes this ark about 450 feet long, 75 feet wide, and 45 feet high.

The Christian Answers Network website offers a contemporary way to look at the cargo capacity of the ark. If you multiply all the measurements together, you have 1,518,750 cubic feet, which is more than the capacity of 569 railroad stock cars. Why did God want the ark to be that large? Why did God want the ark to be 450 feet long, 75 feet wide and 45 feet high? We read in verses 19 and 20 that Noah was supposed to bring into the ark two animals of every kind. If we only look at the types of animals that do not live in the sea, the ark only had the need to carry between forty-five and fifty thousand animals.

Christian Answers Network assumes the average size of an animal on the ark was similar to a sheep. Since 240 sheep can fit into a double-deck railroad stock car, the ark only needed to be about the size of 209 stock cars to carry all the animals (www.christiananswers. net). This means there was lots of room for Noah and his family and extra hay. God provided more than twice as much room as was necessary.

The question is why? Why did God want the ark so large? God wanted Noah to build the ark that large for three reasons. First, He wanted it to take a long, long time to build. It took Noah one hundred years to plan and build the ark. Second, God wanted it to be large enough to hold all the animals, food, and Noah's family. The third and less obvious reason God wanted the ark that large was not for the animals. The third reason was because God wanted to give people plenty of time to repent. God wanted Noah to build a large ark so there would be plenty of room for the animals, plenty of room for food, plenty of room for Noah's family, and plenty of room for all the people who God hoped would repent and join Noah and his family and be saved from the flood. Over the years, as the ark was being built, people had plenty of time to watch Noah, examine their own behavior, repent, and join Noah in living out God's vision.

Faith begins with repentance, declaring our own sinfulness and clinging to the cross of Jesus Christ. As we read in the story of Noah, God will wait and wait and wait for people to repent. One day, however, judgment will come. One day people's lack of faith, lack of obedience, and lack of trusting God will determine their destiny. Just as God prepared plenty of room in the ark, God has also prepared plenty of room at the foot of the cross—plenty of room for people like you and me to find salvation through Jesus Christ. That is why we cannot take the gift of faith and throw it behind the seat like a new pair of gloves. Faith gives us God's vision for our life. It gives us the foundation to be obedient to that vision and, most importantly of all, it attaches us to the cross of Jesus Christ so we can have a relationship with God and receive the gifts of salvation and new life.

Questions

■   How does the sign, "Under New Management,"
describe your relationship with God?

■   What are some benefits from the new management?

■   What was the foundation for Noah's obedience to
God?

■   How did Noah's lifestyle change?

■   If you had been his neighbor, what would you have
thought about Noah?

3

Gift Three

Hope

The LORD then said to Noah, "Go into the ark, you and
your whole family, because I have found you righteous in
this generation. Take with you seven of every kind of clean
animal, a male and its mate, and two of every kind of
unclean animal, a male and its mate, and also seven pairs
of every kind of bird, male and female, to keep their various
kinds alive throughout the earth. Seven days from now I will
send rain on the earth for forty days and forty nights, and I
will wipe from the face of the earth every living creature I
have made."

And Noah did all that the LORD commanded him.

Noah was six hundred years old when the floodwaters
came on the earth. And Noah and his sons and his wife

and his sons' wives entered the ark to escape the waters of the flood. Pairs of clean and unclean animals, of birds and of all creatures that move along the ground, male and female, came to Noah and entered the ark, as God had commanded Noah. And after the seven days the floodwaters came on the earth.

In the six hundredth year of Noah's life, on the seventeenth day of the second month—on that day all the springs of the great deep burst forth, and the floodgates of the heavens were opened. And rain fell on the earth forty days and forty nights.

On that very day Noah and his sons, Shem, Ham and Japheth, together with his wife and the wives of his three sons, entered the ark. They had with them every wild animal according to its kind, all livestock according to their kinds, every creature that moves along the ground according to its kind and every bird according to its kind, everything with wings. Pairs of all creatures that have the breath of life in them came to Noah and entered the ark. The animals going in were male and female of every living thing, as God had commanded Noah. Then the LORD shut him in.

For forty days the flood kept coming on the earth, and as the waters increased they lifted the ark high above the earth. The waters rose and increased greatly on the earth, and the ark floated on the surface of the water.

—Genesis 7:1–18

O n November 20, 1988, at 12:15 a.m., a nineteen-year-old woman was driving her car across a bridge in Los Angeles when she fell asleep at the wheel. The car plunged through a guardrail and was left dangling by its left rear wheel. A half dozen passing motorists stopped, grabbed some ropes from their vehicles, tied the ropes to the back of the woman's car, and hung on until the fire units arrived. A ladder was extended from below to help stabilize the car while firefighters tied the vehicle to two trucks with cables and chains. It took almost two and one half hours for the passers-by, police officers, tow-truck drivers, and firefighters—about twenty-five people in all—to secure the car and pull the woman to safety. After the incident was over, a reporter for the *Los Angeles Times* was interviewing L.A. County Fire Captain, Ross Marshall, and he said, "You know, it was kind of funny. She kept saying, 'I'll do it myself. I'll do it myself.'"

We might laugh at her comments, but at times we think and live the same way when we put all our hope in ourselves. Our life situation will eventually be no better if we put all our hopes in our efforts, in our wisdom or in our experience. If we live life with that kind of hope—hope being a good feeling that things will turn out because of our efforts, wisdom, and experience—then sooner or later we are going to be hanging off a bridge. It might be that our marriage is going to fall apart or we will go through a very discouraging time because we have not been able to

> *Hope means that because God is involved and in control, the situation we are facing will eventually turn out for good.*

free ourselves from our addictions. The question is, how long are you going to say to God, "I'll do it myself. I'll do it myself"?

This third chapter focuses on hope. Through the story of Noah, we discover four reasons why hope is a gift we can't afford to lose.

First, hope is a gift because hope gives us confidence in God.

Hope is not a feeling that things will turn out for the best. Rather, hope is a confidence at the deepest level of our being that God is involved, and that He is in control. Hope means that because God is involved and in control, the situation we are facing will eventually turn out for good, and God will receive the glory.

In Genesis 7:1 we read, *"The Lord then said to Noah, 'Go into the ark, you and your whole family, because I have found you righteous in this generation.'"*

If we just read that sentence casually, we might not understand the full impact of what is written in the story. In Genesis 6:14, God spoke to Noah and gave him the vision of the ark. At that time, Noah was five hundred years old. In Genesis 7:1, God spoke to Noah again. By this time the ark was complete, and Noah was six hundred years old. One hundred years had passed since Noah had heard God speak, and Noah worked on the ark the entire time. Noah heard God speak the vision one time, and Noah altered his life to participate in God's vision. This is not a statement of Noah's ability. More importantly, it is a statement of Noah's confidence in the person who spoke. Noah's confidence was in God. In fact, he had so much confidence in God that it changed Noah's entire life.

Several years ago, my family and I toured the Corvette factory and museum in Bowling Green, Kentucky. What an incredible day!

Touring the factory was fabulous, because I had never seen an automobile assembly line up close. There were about twenty people in our group. Near the end of the tour I stopped to ask one of the guides a question while the rest of the group went to the next stop on the tour. The guide was pleasant and answered my question very thoroughly. When I rejoined the group, a General Motors employee was standing in front of our group with a key in his hand. He had just finished asking a question, but I got there too late to hear what the question was. Our group was silent. Finally, the GM employee asked, "Anybody? Doesn't anybody want to take this key and start that Corvette for the very first time?"

It's amazing how many tremendous opportunities we miss in life because we don't have confidence in the person who speaks.

I was in shock. I could not believe what I was hearing. Was this a joke or was this the chance of a lifetime? He was offering the chance to sit in a new Corvette and be the first one to turn the key. I stood there motionless, speechless. Did I not believe the man who was asking? Did I not have confidence in what he was saying to me? He finally just put the key in someone's hand and said, "Why don't you just go do it?"

It's amazing how many tremendous opportunities we miss in life because we don't have confidence in the person who speaks. I wonder how often the person who has spoken to us has been God.

Second, hope is a gift because hope gives us confidence that God is our partner in life to accomplish His vision.

Let's look again at the story of Noah in Genesis 7:2–4:

"Take with you seven pairs of every kind of clean animal, a male and its mate, and two of every kind of unclean animal, a male and its mate, and also seven pairs of every kind of bird, male and female, to keep their various kinds alive throughout the earth. Seven days from now I will send rain on the earth for forty days and forty nights, and I will wipe from the face of the earth every living creature I have made."

What we read is that the ark had been completed, and God gave Noah instructions about the type and the amount of animals that were to be taken into the ark. Noah followed those instructions, and then God told Noah it was going to rain for forty days and forty nights. In verse 7, Noah and his family got into the ark, and all the animals were gathered together by God into the ark. Then God shut the door of the ark. In verse 17, it began to rain, and rain, and rain. At the very end of verse 18, it had rained enough to lift the giant ark and it began to float on the surface of the water.

As we read this Scripture it is very important to understand the sequence of events that took place in this story. Then we can better understand the gift of hope.

Let's begin with Genesis 7:7. We read these words, *"And Noah and his sons and his wife and his sons' wives entered the ark to escape the waters of the flood."* The question is this: if Noah and his entire family were already in the ark, who remained on the outside of the ark and gathered the animals? Who gathered animals from every geographical region and brought them to the ark? Do you know who was out there? God was out there. God was out there and gathered up the animals and brought them to Noah. Let's go back to chapter 6, verse 20. God told Noah, *"Two of every kind of bird, of every kind of animal and of every kind of creature that moves along the ground **will come to you to be kept alive***" (emphasis added). Those last eight words are so important. Those words tell us that God was going to gather animals and bring them to Noah. That same concept is repeated twice in Genesis 7. First, in Chapter 7:8–9, we read, *"Pairs of clean and unclean animals, of birds and of all creatures that move along the ground, male and female, **came to Noah** and entered the ark, as God had commanded Noah"* (emphasis added).

Second, in chapter 7:15, *"Pairs of all creatures that have the breath of life in them **came to Noah** and entered the ark"* (emphasis added).

Three times within a few paragraphs, the story reveals to us the exact same truth: God gathered the animals and brought them to Noah on the ark. Most of us have the concept that Noah not only had the job of building the ark, but also the job of gathering all the animals. What an impossible task for Noah to fulfill! Noah probably did not know all the animals, birds, and creatures that existed. Adam knew all the animals, birds, and creatures because he named them all. However, generations later, as the animals and birds scattered around the world, it would have been impossible for Noah to know all of them and gather them in one place.

What we read in the Scripture is that God gave Noah the vision to build the ark. God gave him the patience and the endurance and all of the wood to build the ark. That was Noah's job. It was also Noah's job to gather food for the animals. However, it was God's job to provide the animals. They worked in partnership. Noah did what he could do and God did what Noah could not do, and together a miracle happened. That is where hope comes in. Hope gives us the confidence that God will be our partner in life to accomplish His vision.

It is important for us to understand that **Noah did what he could do and God did what Noah could not do**, and together they worked in partnership, each depending on the other to fulfill his part. This story of Noah is not the only place in the Bible where God worked in partnership and depended upon people to do their part. We see the same dynamic in Matthew 14:28–29. The disciples were out in the boat in the midst of the sea and Jesus walked to them on the water. Peter saw Jesus, and Peter said, *"Lord, if it is you…tell me to come to you on the water.' 'Come,'[Jesus] said. Then Peter got down out of the boat, walked on the water and came toward Jesus"* (Matthew 14:28–29).

It is important to understand what happened in this incident. It is the same dynamic that happened with God and Noah. Peter did what he could do. He walked. It was Jesus who did what Peter could not do and provided the miracle. They worked in partnership together, each depending on the other to do what he could not do.

The same dynamic is in the Gospel of John's story of the raising of Lazarus from the dead. After Lazarus had been dead four days, Jesus came to the tomb and wept. People waited to see what Jesus would do. Jesus went to the tomb and looked down on the tomb with the stone laying across it (John 11:38), He turned to His disciples and said, *"Take away the stone"* (John 11:39).

Why did Jesus ask the disciples to move the stone? He certainly did not need their help. After all, there were no humans to move the stone from Christ's tomb on Easter morning. Jesus asked them because He wanted them to do what they could do to be partners with Him in providing new life. Then Jesus did what they could not do—raise Lazarus from the dead.

When Lazarus came from the tomb, Jesus again turned to His disciples and said, *"Take off the grave clothes and let him go"* (John 11:44). Why did Jesus want the disciples to unbind Lazarus? No one helped Jesus unbind Himself from His grave clothes. Again, Jesus was depending upon human beings to do what they could do.

This same dynamic happens over and over again throughout the Bible. God wants to work in partnership with humankind. He challenges us to do what we can do, so He will do what we cannot do; together in partnership, miracles happen. It is this partnership that we read about in Genesis Chapter 7 with the building of the ark and the gathering of the animals. Noah did what he could do. He built the ark and gathered the food. God did what Noah could not do. He provided the animals. We cannot afford to lose the gift of hope because hope gives us the confidence that God will be our partner in life to accomplish His vision. With that hope, we do our part, knowing God will do His part.

Sometimes we believe God is taking from us instead of partnering with us. When we believe this, we do not allow ourselves to see or experience God's compassion for us. The following story, based on Valerie Cox's poem "The Cookie Thief," illustrates this point. A woman was waiting for her plane at an airport and she got hungry. She folded the newspaper she was reading, placed it under her arm and walked over to the little store in the airport and bought a package of cookies. Then she went back to her seat and began reading her newspaper. After a few minutes she thought, "I might as well start eating my cookies." So she reached down, got a cookie and ate it. About a minute later, she heard a rustling in her newspaper. She looked down and saw a hand under her paper. The hand took one of her cookies and disappeared. She thought, "Well, that's kind of strange. I wonder who that is." She got another cookie and ate it. Thirty seconds later, she saw the hand under her newspaper again. This hand took another cookie and disappeared. By then there was only one cookie left. The hand appeared again and reached for the cookies. It took the last cookie, broke that cookie in two and slid the half over to this woman. Then the other half of the cookie disappeared with the hand. When this happened, the lady put down her newspaper and saw a man eating half of the cookie. Then he stood up and walked off. This made the woman furious. Why would this man eat her cookies? How rude could he be! Right then, she heard the announcement that her plane was boarding. She folded her newspaper and put it under her arm. She walked over to the boarding gate where she was to give her ticket to the flight attendant. She unzipped her purse and looked inside. Do you know what she found? Her own package of cookies!

Many times, that same dynamic exists in our relationship with God. We assume that God is taking from us that which is ours. In reality, the truth is that God wants to be in partnership with us to bring miracles and blessings to people. Unfortunately, we live much of our lives without ever realizing it. Hope is a gift we can't afford to lose because hope gives us the confidence that God is our partner in life to accomplish His vision.

Third, hope is a gift because hope gives us confidence that God provides direction in our life.

Let's turn back to Genesis: *"So make yourself an ark of cypress wood; make rooms in it and coat it with pitch inside and out. This is how you shall build it: The ark is to be 450 feet long, 75 feet wide and 45 feet high. Make a roof for it and finish the ark to within 18 inches of the top. Put a door in the side of the ark and make lower, middle, and upper decks"* (Genesis 6:14–16).

That's the entire description of the ark. If we are familiar with boats, we will notice quickly that two very important items are missing from the ark. The ark had no rudder and no oars or paddles. There was no way to steer it and no way to power it. Once the flood waters came, everything was encased inside of the ark. Once the ark began to float upon the waters, it simply moved across the face of the waters being totally steered by the hand of God. Noah had to totally depend upon God to provide the right direction for his life.

Several months ago, I was fishing with a man by the name of Hershel. We went down to a lake near Ennis, Texas. We started fishing about 6:00 p.m. and fished until the middle of the night. I had never been on that lake before, so when it got dark I had no idea where we were. We were fishing in total darkness. There were a few lights from fishing piers and we were fishing around those piers. Finally, we decided it was time to go home, and Hershel turned to me and said these words, "Dean, do you want to take the boat in?" I said, "What?" He said, "Do you want to drive the boat in?" I said, "No, if it was during the day, it would be fine, but I

41

don't want to take the risk at night." Well, Hershel started the engine, drove the boat about 50 yards, turned to the right and we were at the boat dock!

Hope is a gift we can't afford to lose because hope gives us the confidence that God will provide direction in our lives.

So many times in life, it is just like on that boat. We are so close to our destination, and we don't even realize it until we allow God to provide direction for our life. As you read this book, do you need direction for a decision you are making? Do you feel like you are all alone? God will provide direction if we let Him. Hope is a gift we can't afford to lose because hope gives us the confidence that God will provide direction in our lives.

Fourth, hope is a gift because hope gives us the confidence that God will always provide a way of escape.

We read these words in 1 Corinthians 10:13: *"No temptation has seized you except what is common to man. And God is faithful; He will not let you to be tempted beyond what you can bear. But when you are tempted, He will also provide a way out so that you can stand up under it."*

God is committed to providing a way of escape. That is exactly what He was doing in the story of Noah and the ark. God provided the way of escape. Not just for Noah, but also for his family and the animals. The reason the ark was so large was because God wanted to have room for other people in addition to Noah. One reason it took so long to build the ark is because God waited for people to repent. God gave people a way of escape.

God will do the same for you and for me. God will provide a way to escape the guilt and the shame that comes when we sin against God. Look at 1 John 1:9 where we read these words: *"If we confess our sins, He is faithful and just and will forgive us our sins and purify us from all unrighteousness."*

It is important to understand that the way of escape is confession and clinging to the cross of Jesus Christ.

The object that allowed Noah and his family to escape the tragedy was made of wood. That is no coincidence. In the New Testament the object which allows you and me to escape from guilt and shame is also made of wood. One was an ark, one was a cross. Both provide ways of escape and both were provided by God.

During the reign of King Frederick II, the king visited a prison in Berlin, Germany. As he walked through the dungeon prison, he walked by all of the prisoners and looked into every cell. As he did, each one would reach their hands through the bars, speak to the king, and try to convince him of their innocence. He walked up and down each aisle and each prisoner, one after the other, would say the same thing. Finally he came to one of the last cells in the prison. The man in that cell did not reach his hands through the bars and did not declare his innocence. Rather, that one man sat in the corner on his bed with his knees to his chest and his face down. The king stopped, looked, and asked this man, "Sir, why are you in prison?" The man looked up and recognized the king and said, "Your majesty, I am in here for armed robbery." The king turned to him and said, "Are you guilty?" The man said, "Yes, sir, I have no excuse," hanging his head in shame. The king turned to the guards and said, "Release this guilty man. I do not want him corrupting all of these innocent people." The same thing is true in our lives when we confess our sins to the King of kings and Lord of lords. He will not condemn us and leave us in the prison of our sin. He will set us free through the cross of Jesus Christ. He will free us for new life and provide a way of escape from our guilt and our shame.

> *I challenge you to cling to the cross and walk away with confidence that God through His Son Jesus Christ will provide the way of escape. I challenge you to welcome God's involvement in your life. I challenge you to choose to be God's partner. I challenge you to allow God to provide direction in your life.*

Is that what you need today? Do you need to have the confidence that God will provide a way of escape from the life you have been living to a new life of freedom, truth, honesty, and integrity? Hope is that gift that gives us the confidence that God will be our partner, that God will give direction in our life, and that God will provide a way of escape. Right now, God is providing that way of escape for you to escape a life of sin, to escape a life of dissatisfaction, to escape a life of empty promises and broken dreams. He is challenging you to accept the gift of hope.

Right now, I challenge you to cling to the cross and walk away with confidence that God, through His Son Jesus Christ, will provide the way of escape. I challenge you to welcome God's involvement in your life. I challenge you to choose to be God's partner. I challenge you to allow God to provide direction in your life. I also challenge you to cling to the cross of Jesus Christ and allow God to provide the way of escape from your guilt and your shame.

At the beginning of the story of Noah, we read these words in Genesis 6:8, *"But Noah found favor in the eyes of the Lord."* That was not just true for Noah. That is also true for you and for me. We, too, have found favor in the eyes of God. The question is, will we accept the gift of grace that will give us faith and hope? There were several remarkable qualities about Noah. He was willing to welcome God's involvement in his life. He welcomed God as his partner in life. He was willing to totally depend upon God for direction in life. He was also willing to totally depend upon God to provide the way of escape. It was all because Noah accepted the gift of hope. For you and me to accept that same gift, we need to accept the gift through the cross of Jesus Christ. I challenge you to cling to the hope that only God can give you.

Questions

- How is our hope influenced by our beliefs regarding God?

- What "tremendous opportunities" have you missed in life because you had trouble believing?

- Who accepted the job to provide the animals in the ark?

- What job is God inviting you to do?

- What job does God want you to believe He will do?

4

Gift Four
Patience

They rose greatly on the earth, and all the high mountains under the entire heavens were covered. The waters rose and covered the mountains to a depth of more than twenty feet. Every living thing that moved on the earth perished—birds, livestock, wild animals, all the creatures that swarm over the earth, and all mankind. Everything on dry land that had the breath of life in its nostrils died. Every living thing on the face of the earth was wiped out; men and animals and the creatures that move along the ground and the birds of the air were wiped from the earth. Only Noah was left, and those with him in the ark.

The waters flooded the earth for a hundred and fifty days.

But God remembered Noah and all the wild animals and the livestock that were with him in the ark, and he sent a wind over the earth, and the waters receded. Now the springs of the deep and the floodgates of the heavens had been closed, and the rain had stopped falling from the sky. The water receded steadily from the earth. At the end of the hundred and fifty days the water had gone down, and on the seventeenth day of the seventh month the ark came to rest on the mountains of Ararat. The waters continued to recede until the tenth month, and on the first day of the tenth month the tops of the mountains became visible.

After forty days Noah opened the window he had made in the ark and sent out a raven, and it kept flying back and forth until the water had dried up from the earth. Then he sent out a dove to see if the water had receded from the surface of the ground. But the dove could find no place to set its feet because there was water over all the surface of the earth; so it returned to Noah in the ark. He reached out his hand and took the dove and brought it back to himself in the ark. He waited seven more days and again sent out the dove from the ark. When the dove returned to him in the evening, there in its beak was a freshly plucked olive leaf! Then Noah knew that the water had receded from the earth. He waited seven more days and sent the dove out again, but this time it did not return to him.

—Genesis 7:19–8:12

Many years ago, a young man by the name of James Lally had a dream of becoming a surgeon just like his father. One of the most exciting days in his life was the day he received his acceptance letter to Northwestern University Medical School. Jim worked hard and did well in medical school. His dreams were coming true.

But at the beginning of Jim's final year at Northwestern, his world suddenly fell apart. Once a year, all medical school students were given routine physical examinations. The medical dean called Jim into his office and told him that he had tuberculosis.

There were no drugs with which to treat TB at that time. There was no way to predict whether a patient would ever recover. The only treatment was to stay in bed for an entire year. Imagine the shock to be within two semesters of becoming a medical doctor and to be cruelly yanked out of school and perhaps out of your career.

Riding home that day on the rattling commuter train was an absolute low point in Jim's life. All his dreams were vanishing. He had been so full of life, but now he did not know whether he would live or die. He was a superior boxer, active in the Catholic youth organization, and in the Golden Gloves. That summer he had taken flying lessons early each morning, and then would hurry into Chicago to work all day at a medical laboratory. He loved his work. After work, he attended school each evening before returning home again. Now all his activity was over. As a medical student, he knew what would happen to him in the future. As he lay month after month in bed, his body would become flabby and his muscles would lose their tone. Those first few weeks were difficult, especially when his medical school friends stopped by to tell him what they were doing and learning. He sunk into despair.

It was at this point in his life that Jim learned one of the most valuable lessons that any one of us could ever learn. He learned the importance of patience. He also learned how easy it is to become negative while we wait. He realized that while we wait and wait, for whatever reason, we have a choice to make. It is the choice to either be negative or positive. If we choose to be negative, that is called whining. If we choose to be positive, that is called patience. In the midst of this decision-making process, Jim's mother helped him realize that a choice to be positive was a choice for courage instead of despondency. It was a choice for self-control, not self-pity.

In the midst of his waiting, Jim struggled with that decision, the same decision that you and I struggle with. Jim made a decision for patience, courage, and self-control. When he made a decision for patience, he made a decision against negativity and despondency and self-pity. Almost immediately after he made that decision, he made another decision. It was a decision to begin a yearlong reading program. He began to read medical books, medical journals, and, for a change of pace, he read every word that Shakespeare ever wrote. Jim re-entered medical school one year later, physically weak and out of condition. However, due to his year of reading he was well-prepared for his courses. He found the time to exercise and strengthen his body. During his year of waiting, Jim learned a lesson that I would like to share with you in this chapter. It is the lesson that patience is a gift we can't afford to lose.

Noah, his family, and all the animals also went through a year-long waiting period. In fact, they were in the ark for more than a year. They were in the ark for 375 days. The phrase, "God give me patience, and do it right now!" comes to my mind. God was going to do for Noah, just not quickly. Remember the word again: patience.

This story can teach us three important lessons about patience.

First, patience is a gift because patience teaches us to trust God's timing, not ours.

In Genesis 7:11–12 we read that it began to rain: *"In the six hundredth year of Noah's life, on the seventeenth day of the second month—on that day, all the springs of the great deep burst forth, and the floodgates of the heavens were opened. And rain fell on the earth forty days and forty nights."*

We might be wondering why the writer was so specific to tell us the year, the month, and the date of each one of these events. I believe it is to help us to understand how long Noah was in the ark. In Genesis 7:11 the rain began. Five months later, the ark rested on Mount Ararat. In Genesis 8:4, the ark rested in the seventeenth day of the seventh month on the mountains of Ararat. In Genesis 8:5, two and a half months later, the mountains were seen and the waters decreased continually until the tenth month. Then, on the first day of the tenth month, the tops of the mountains were seen. Forty days later, Noah opened the window of the ark and sent out a raven and a dove. Seven days later, he sent out a dove again and it returned with an olive branch. Seven days later, he sent out the dove a third time and it did not return. Noah waited forty more days until he removed the covering of the ark. Then fifty-one days later, God told Noah that everyone could leave the ark.

The main reason this story is so specific about the length of days for each event is to help us understand how long Noah and the others were in the ark. When we count up all the days from the beginning of the rain until the time the ark was vacated, it adds up to 375 days. See **Chart 1: Days in the Ark** (on the next page).

Why did it rain for forty days and take 335 days for all the water to recede? We see some of that same dynamic in this country when it rains for two to three days and takes weeks for the water to recede. In the midst of those days, I believe God was teaching Noah to trust in God's timing, not his.

Let me share two stories about why God's timing, not ours, is so important. Several years ago, I went to Russia and Latvia on a mission trip. Each person was assigned a translator; mine was a woman named Agnese. These two stories come out of my second week while I was in Latvia. They happened on the same day in the city of Riga. I had been working in Riga for three days and we had a free evening on a Wednesday night. My roommate, Stan, and I wanted to take our translators out to eat as a way of thanking them for all the help they had given us. They said they would love to go out to dinner. They taught an English class in their home from 5:30 p.m. to 6:30 p.m., so they would meet us in downtown Old Riga at 7:00 p.m. Stan and I took the trolley bus to downtown Riga. We had about an hour and a half to walk around and see the sights, and then we were to meet our translators in front of the Hotel Riga at 7:00 p.m.

At 7:00, Stan and I were walking toward the front entrance of Hotel Riga, when from a distance of about 75 feet we saw our translators standing there waiting for us. During the day, our translators dressed very conservatively. However, when they went home, they obviously went home to do more than just teach an English class. They had also changed their clothes. The moment that Stan and I

Chart 1
Days in the Ark

Noah was 600 years old when the flood waters came.
(Genesis 7:6)

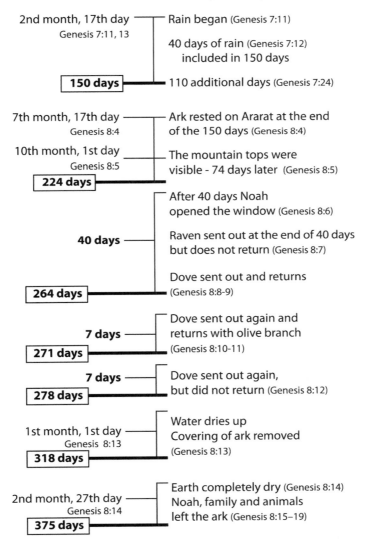

2nd month, 17th day — Rain began (Genesis 7:11)
Genesis 7:11, 13

40 days of rain (Genesis 7:12)
included in 150 days

150 days — 110 additional days (Genesis 7:24)

7th month, 17th day — Ark rested on Ararat at the end
Genesis 8:4 — of the 150 days (Genesis 8:4)

10th month, 1st day — The mountain tops were
Genesis 8:5 — visible - 74 days later (Genesis 8:5)
224 days

After 40 days Noah
opened the window (Genesis 8:6)

40 days — Raven sent out at the end of 40 days
but does not return (Genesis 8:7)

Dove sent out and returns
264 days — (Genesis 8:8-9)

Dove sent out again and
7 days — returns with olive branch
271 days — (Genesis 8:10-11)

Dove sent out again,
7 days — but did not return (Genesis 8:12)
278 days

Water dries up
1st month, 1st day — Covering of ark removed
Genesis 8:13 — (Genesis 8:13)
318 days

Earth completely dry (Genesis 8:14)
2nd month, 27th day — Noah, family and animals
Genesis 8:14 — left the ark (Genesis 8:15–19)
375 days

Total: 1 year, 10 days (375 days assuming 1 month = 30 days long) saw these two women, we looked at each other—our eyes as big as saucers. We were shocked to notice, even from a distance, what they were **not** wearing! We approached our translators very cautiously. When we got to where they were standing, the four of us began talking there in a circle. Since we did not know any of the restaurants in Riga, Stan and I asked the translators to choose a restaurant. Right in the middle of this conversation, I was thinking to myself, "How in the world are we going to get out of this predicament, because obviously these girls are thinking that this is more than just dinner! It looks as if they had dressed up for a date (at least)." While I was thinking about that, I was praying. Knowing Stan, he was also praying, trying to figure out how God could get us out of a situation that we had unknowingly gotten ourselves into. We didn't tell anyone that we were going to Old Riga, and we did not know anyone else from our group who was going to Old Riga that night. As the four of us were standing there, we made a decision about the restaurant. We turned around and right in front of us were three other people from our group. Both Stan and I, at the same time, gave a big sigh of relief. I don't like to put myself into those types of uncomfortable situations. If we had left even a minute before, chances are we would never have met anyone else from the group, but God's timing in the midst of our waiting was just perfect.

The seven of us had dinner that night and then at about 10:00 p.m., we walked our translators to the train station so they could take the train home. Then, the five of us began to walk back to the bus stop so we could take the trolley bus back to our dorm. The sun was just about to go down, and we were walking by one of the parks in Riga, when all of a sudden from the right came a cry, "Stan!

Dean!" We turned and there were two women from our group who came running toward us, their faces full of tears, and they said to us, "We came down to have dinner and we got lost; we have been walking around for more than an hour, trying to find our way back." The seven of us stopped there in the middle of the sidewalk on the edge of that park, and we said a prayer of thanksgiving to God, for His timing had been perfect once again. Patience is a gift because patience teaches us to trust God's timing, not our own.

Second, patience is a gift because patience teaches us to trust God's plan for our life and not our plan.

When we learn to trust God's plan we learn to trust that what is happening *in* us is greater than what is happening *to* us. Several years ago, I went to my twentieth high school reunion in Albuquerque, New Mexico. Before I went to the reunion, I got out my old high school yearbook and began to flip through all of the pages. On the very last page, I came across a short note that was written by a girl named Sharon. I do not remember Sharon, but this is what she wrote, "Dean, I don't know what to say but I'll try. I'm really glad I got to know you. I hope I do get to know you better. You'll have to come by 'cause I don't know where you live. Gee, I'm really sorry that things didn't work out too good for you this year, but I'm sure things will be different in the years to come. You are a really far-out guy, stay that way. That's all, life does have a purpose. This doesn't make sense, oh, well. Good luck, Love, Sharon."

She wrote those words many years ago, and if I look back on my senior year today, the question I have to ask is what is she talking about? What does she mean that things didn't work out for me that year? I remember my senior year as one of the best years of my life. I had a girlfriend, finally, that lasted more than a week. I got accepted to Baylor University. At the end of my junior year, I had become a Christian and as a senior had gotten very involved in my youth group. I lettered in tennis for the third straight year. I had worked through the school year and that summer, and I had bought my first car. In the midst of all those little things that happen in life, I wonder if I was more concerned about what was happening *to* me than what was happening *in* me.

God's desire for our life is that we become more like His Son Jesus. That requires God working in us to transform our mind, change our heart, rearrange our priorities, and establish new habits and discipline. God is committed to our transformation and He hopes on a daily basis that we are also.

If you want to know and live God's vision for your life, and if you want to be the greatest blessing possible to others, then focus upon what happens in you.

Too often it is easier to focus on what happens *to* us rather than what happens *in* us. God is so committed to the transformation of what is in us because what is inside will eventually show itself outside. This transformation takes time. It is not instantaneous. It is the difference between cooking a roast in the crock pot and cooking a roast in the microwave. If we just want to heat the roast, a microwave will work fine. However, if we want to fully permeate the food with flavor and tenderize every bite, a crock pot makes all the difference.

The same dynamic is true in life. If you want to live from day to day without worrying about God's bigger picture of you, then simply focus upon what happens *to* you. However, if you want to know and live God's vision for your life, and if you want to be the greatest blessing possible to others, then focus upon what happens *in* you.

This does not mean become self-centered. It means to become Christ-centered and allow the character, words, and actions of Christ to penetrate everything you do. Becoming Christ-centered will take time, but during this time we will also learn to trust God's purpose and plan for our life instead of our own plan.

The reason patience is such an important gift of God is because it teaches us to trust God's purpose and plan instead of our own. It teaches us to trust that what is happening in us is greater than what is happening to us.

A familiar joke illustrates this point. Two rich brothers were members of one church and suddenly one of them passed away. Neither brother was known for his moral or ethical purity. The church had just built a brand-new building and the remaining brother went to the young preacher and said, "Now here is an envelope with enough money to pay off the entire building, if tomorrow during the funeral you will say that my brother was a saint."

That was a difficult choice for the preacher to make. The young preacher finally agreed and took the money. The next day during the funeral, the young preacher got up and he said these words, "This man was a liar, he was a cheat, he was unethical, he cheated on his wife, but compared to his brother, this man was a saint."

God's goal for you and me in this life is for us to be saints. A saint is simply a person through whom the light of Jesus Christ shines. In our lives, the light of Jesus shines brighter when we focus on what is happening *in* us more than what is happening *to* us. In order to do that, we really need to trust God's plan for our life, not our plan.

In the book of Genesis, Noah and his family were closed up in the ark for more than one year. In the midst of that year, I am sure that they began to ask the question of why. Why is it taking so long? What is happening out there? Why doesn't God do something? In the midst of those questions, many times we don't understand. However, the true question is this: In the midst of those times when we don't understand, are we still willing to trust God's plan for our lives? You see, patience is a gift of the faithfulness of God because it teaches us to trust God's plan and not our plan.

Diana and I were married while I was in seminary. We wanted to have children when I finished, but it just did not happen. We realized that God's creativity doesn't always work according to our time line. We went through infertility testing. Diana had two operations—still nothing. We put our name on the adoption list at the Methodist Mission Home in San Antonio. We wanted a child whether we were the biological parents or not. Finally, after almost three years of testing and surgery, Diana got pregnant and Matt was born in March 1984. Why didn't it happen before then? Why doesn't that happen to every couple in that situation? I can't explain God's timing or His plan. But the question is—do I trust God's plan or not?

In Genesis 12:1, God gave Abraham a vision of being a great nation and he had no children. He was seventy-five years old then. In Genesis 15:1–5, Abraham still had no son and God repeated His plan and promise. In Genesis 16, Abraham took God's plan into his own hands and had a son by Hagar. In Genesis 17, Abraham was ninety-nine years old and it was twenty-four years after God's first promise. In Genesis 21, Isaac was born—twenty-five years after God first spoke to Abraham. Why twenty-five years? I can't explain God's timing or plan. Maybe it is because Rebekah had not yet been born. I don't know. From the time we receive God's plan until His plan finds fulfillment, obedience is necessary.

In obedience we can be negative or positive. When we are negative it is called whining. When we are positive it is called patience. Patience helps us trust God's plan, not ours.

Third, patience is a gift because patience teaches us to trust God's presence and not our circumstances.

In the book of Genesis, there is something very important in this story that is not recorded during the 375 days that Noah and his family were in the ark. At the beginning of this story (Genesis 6:14), we read that God spoke to Noah about the ark. We also read in chapter 6 that God spoke to Noah about the type of animals to bring into the ark. In chapter 7, we read that God spoke to Noah and told Noah to go into the ark. In chapter 8, we read that God spoke to Noah and told him to come out of the ark. Then in chapter 9, after all that took place, we read that God spoke to Noah and gave him the rainbow.

In the midst of life's storms, in the midst of life's traumas, why is it that sometimes we feel that God is so absent? Why do we feel that God has abandoned us? I believe it is during those times that God wants us to trust in His presence more than our circumstances.

What is important is something that is not recorded. During these 375 days of Noah actually being closed up in the ark, not one time is it recorded that God spoke to Noah. The question we need to ask ourselves is why? Why did God speak to Noah before he went into the ark? Why did God speak to Noah after he came out of the ark? But why did God *not* speak to Noah while he was in the ark? Have you ever wondered that about your own life? In the midst of life's storms, in the midst of life's traumas, why is it that sometimes we feel that God is so absent? Why do we feel that God has abandoned us? I believe it is during those times that God wants us to trust in His presence more than our circumstances.

Circumstances are like a mattress. When we're on top, we rest in comfort. However, when we're underneath, we can get smothered, unless we realize that when we are underneath our circumstances, we are not alone; God is with us. Patience teaches us to trust in God's presence, not our circumstances. The great teacher, Charles Spurgeon, was teaching a class of young seminary students on the fine points of preaching. He said, "When you speak of heaven, let your face light up and be radiant with a heavenly gleam; let your eyes shine with reflected glory. But when you speak of hell, well then, your everyday face will do." What do our everyday faces tell other people? Do they tell other people that we are trusting in God's presence more than our circumstances?

Do you trust God's plan for your life instead of your own? Do you trust God's timing in life more than your own timing in life?

A woman from our church who was in her mid-forties was diagnosed with cancer. She was home in bed and her parents were taking care of her. At times she seemed to get worse. At times she just seemed to hang on. Once when I visited her, I sat next to her bed and served her Holy Communion. As we were talking, she slowly reached out and took my hand and said, "Dean, don't worry about me; I still believe in miracles." Then she smiled. That smile radiated a message to me that in the midst of her darkest night, in the midst of a time when she had been shut up in an ark like Noah, in the midst of a time when she could ask the question, "Where is God?" she had learned that patience is trusting God's presence, not our circumstances.

What about you? Do you trust in God's presence more than your circumstances? Do you trust God's plan for your life instead of your own? Do you trust God's timing in life more than your own timing in life? If you do, then you have learned that patience is a gift from the faithfulness of God. Television channel eight in Dallas has a great commercial about the weather. On this commercial, you see a storm, lightning, and the wind. Then you hear this voice, "When you can't trust the weather, trust in the weatherman." Isn't that what God was trying to teach Noah during those 375 days in the ark? Isn't that what God is trying to teach you and me? When we can't trust the circumstances around us, we can trust the One who is greater than our circumstances. Jesus Christ has not abandoned us in the midst of our darkness. He is right there. We

> *When we can't trust the circumstances around us, we can trust the One who is greater than our circumstances.*

must have patience and trust in God's timing, not ours; trust in His plan and not ours; trust in His presence and not our circumstances.

One of the most powerful experiences I have ever encountered about trusting God happened while I was at Baylor University. One of the people I knew at Baylor was a woman by the name of Dottie Robinson. While we were in college, she wanted to go on a mission trip with the Baptist Student Union. Dottie prayed about it and felt that God had given her a vision to work on this mission trip and she was really, really excited. Each and every day that the trip got closer, her hope was building. The problem was that she did not have the money. Her family situation was such that they could just barely afford to pay for her schooling, and she really had no extra money. So we began to pray that if it was God's plan for her to go on this mission trip, He would provide the money. I do not remember the exact dollar amount that she needed; it was around $700. Up until the day before the trip, Dottie only had $100. In the midst of all the circumstances, we tried to still be positive, even though she had only one more day to turn in her money. I remember the morning we met in one of the dorms and prayed together, "God, we know it is possible for You to do this. We don't know how it is going to work, but if it's Your desire that she do this, if this is truly something You plan on her doing, then would You please, in Your miraculous way, provide for her?"

We had breakfast. I sat with her again at lunch. Nothing had happened. I sat with her at dinner. Nothing had happened. She was supposed to turn in the money that night by midnight. About 9:30 p.m. there was a knock on her door. She opened the door and there was a girl she had never met who said, "I've heard about the fact that you want to go on the mission trip and that you don't have any money. Here, I will help you go." She gave Dottie $20. Dottie was so excited, even though she still had hundreds of dollars yet to raise. Five minutes later the same thing happened, and again in another five minutes. It seemed as if every few minutes, people she had never met began to arrive and shower her with money. She called me about 11:00 p.m. and began to tell me what was happening. She had to put the phone down to go answer the door. All of her visitors were girls who lived there in her dorm, who just kept coming by and bringing money. With about 20 minutes to go, the last few dollars came in.

It is so easy to look at our circumstances instead of God's presence.

What a great lesson on patience! In the midst of life, in the midst of those dark times when we are closed off in the midst of a storm, it is so easy not to have patience. It is so easy to trust in our timing and not God's. It is so easy to trust in our plan and not God's. It is so easy to look at our circumstances instead of God's presence. Patience is what Dottie and I learned that night, among many other things.

Patience is a gift from God. It teaches us to trust in God's timing, not ours. It teaches us to trust in God's plan, not our plan. It teaches us to trust in His presence more than our circumstances. Is that what you need right now? Do you need to recommit yourself to the One who is greater than your circumstances? Do you need to recommit yourself to the One who has a plan for your life, and to the One who can see the big picture of what is going on and not just the moment? There is only one who can give you that gift of patience. His name is Jesus.

Questions

■ What thoughts come to your mind when you hear the word "patience?"

■ How does that word relate to Noah and the ark?

■ What do you think of God's timing in the midst of our waiting?

■ How can you improve your willingness to wait with patience while trusting God's timing?

Gift Five

Worship

By the first day of the first month of Noah's six hundred and first year, the water had dried up from the earth. Noah then removed the covering from the ark and saw that the surface of the ground was dry. By the twenty-seventh day of the second month the earth was completely dry.

Then God said to Noah, "Come out of the ark, you and your wife and your sons and their wives. Bring out every kind of living creature that is with you—the birds, the animals, and all the creatures that move along the ground—so they can multiply on the earth and be fruitful and increase in number upon it."

So Noah came out, together with his sons and his wife and his sons' wives. All the animals and all the creatures that move *along the ground and all the birds—everything that moves on the earth—came out of the ark, one kind after another.*

*Then Noah built an altar to the L*ORD *and, taking some of all the clean animals and clean birds, he sacrificed burnt offerings on it. The L*ORD *smelled the pleasing aroma and said in his heart: "Never again will I curse the ground because of man, even though every inclination of his heart is evil from childhood. And never again will I destroy all living creatures, as I have done.*

"As long as the earth endures, seedtime and harvest, cold and heat, summer and winter, day and night will never cease."

—Genesis 8:13–22

S everal years ago our son, Matt, and I hiked to the top of Pike's Peak. We trained for a year, riding bicycles and hiking with backpacks about once a month. He was using the miles to earn his hiking badge in the Boy Scouts. I walked with him because of a promise I made and just to be with him. Even though we had walked 20 miles one Saturday to prepare for the Peak, nothing we could do in the Dallas/Fort Worth area could prepare us for the change in altitude we would experience on that day.

We did not hike alone. A friend and medical doctor, Charlie Balzaldua, hiked with us. Charlie and his family had moved to Colorado Springs the year before. An avid hiker, he was acclimated to the altitude we faced that day.

The plan was to begin at 5:00 a.m. and reach the summit by noon. My wife, Diana, daughter, Trisha, and Charlie's wife, Susan, planned to ride the cog train up the mountain mid-morning, meet us at the top at noon, then we'd all ride the train down about 1:00 p.m. They had to buy our return tickets or we would not have had a ride off the mountain.

We began our ascent up the Barr Trail just as planned. We reached the halfway point at Barr Camp right on schedule and without any difficulty. After a few minutes of rest, we began again. Before long the trail became steeper and harder. Quickly, I learned that I was carrying too much in my pack. Charlie changed packs with me and carried the heavier pack. While Matt and Charlie seemed to be fine, I frequently stopped to rest and catch my breath. Time was ticking away and we were behind schedule. The climb became harder and harder with each step.

With a mile to go we saw the summit! I also heard the train and looked at my watch. It was 1:00 p.m. That was our train leaving and we were not on it. There was nothing I could do but slowly put one foot in front of another. At that point in the trail there is a geological formation called the 16 Golden Stairs. I do not remember how long it took me to climb those stairs, but Charlie and Matt were pushing and pulling me every step of the way.

At the top of the stairs I had to rest. All of a sudden a man I had never met before came down the trail. He stopped, pointed his finger at me and said, "You're Dean Posey."

"Yes," I said, "How did you know that?"

He said, "Your wife is up on the top of the mountain worried about you. She asked if I was going down the trail and I said, 'Yes.'

She asked if I would look for you to make sure you were okay. I told her I would and asked how I would recognize you. She told me that I was to look for a bald man with a young boy."

We did make it to the summit soon after this encounter.

But this is the lesson. Diana, who was on the top of the mountain used a messenger to communicate her concern for me. The same dynamic happened with God the Father and His Son, Jesus. God the Father who is up in heaven sent His Son, Jesus, down to earth to be a messenger of the Father's love. Every time we worship, whether privately or publicly, we get reconnected to the Messenger.

This chapter focuses upon the gift of worship. From the story of Noah, we discover four reasons why this gift of worship is a gift we can't afford to lose.

First, worship is a gift because worship helps us declare that our highest loyalty is to the eternal, not the temporal.

In Genesis 8:16, God told Noah to come out of the ark. In Genesis 8:20, we read that the first thing Noah did after he came out of the ark was *"build an altar to the Lord"* and worship. The question is why? Why do that first? When Noah got out of the ark, there were so many things he could have done first. Everything had been washed away. If Noah's wife made any sort of "honey-do" list, I am sure it was a long one.

He needed to find a home. He needed to provide for his family again. He had spent the last one hundred years before the flood building an ark, what was he going to do now? Imagine going through a midlife crisis at 601 years of age! Though Noah lived 349 more years, it is hard to think of how he felt then. There were so many things he could do. But nothing was more important in his life at that moment than to worship and to declare that his highest loyalty was to the eternal, not the temporal.

Why is it so difficult these days to follow Noah's example? Why does the temporal crowd out our time for the eternal?

Another adventure Matt and I experienced was the Hotter 'N Hell Hundred bicycle race in Wichita Falls, Texas. The H3—as it is known to Texans—is held the weekend before Labor Day each year and normally attracts about ten thousand cyclists from all over the world. With the race being held in August, it has earned its name. Participants do not have to ride 100 miles. There is also the option of riding 25 miles, 50 miles, or 100 kilometers (62.5 miles). Since it was a few months after Pikes Peak, we chose to ride the 100 kilometers.

The weather forecast was for thunderstorms and rain. We had to make a decision before the race even started: if it begins to rain, and the road becomes slick and the riding conditions become unsafe, what were we going to do? Did we go all that way just to stop and have the truck haul us back to the starting line? My wife, Diana, would have said, "Yes! That's exactly what you need to do."

However, Matt and I made a decision without ever verbalizing it to each other. That decision was that no matter what, we did not train that long or travel that far only to finish half the race. So we rode 100 kilometers. It sprinkled on us for about five minutes at the 45 mile point, but we were ready. We had our ponchos. We were ready at any moment to pull them out, put them on, and keep riding.

I wonder how similar that dynamic is to worship. I wonder how many of us approach God and say no matter how stormy life gets, we will still choose to worship Him? I wonder how many of us approach God and say no matter what happens in life, no matter what You can see and we can't, no matter how unsafe it might appear, no matter how physically challenging the course of life might get, we will still choose to worship You—to stay the course and finish the race.

Worship is a gift of God because worship helps us declare that our highest loyalty is to the eternal, not the temporal. One of these days, you and I will be in a position where the temporal is gone and only the eternal is left. Unlike Noah, it will not be the moment we come out of an ark. Rather, it will be the moment we pass from this life to the next. Since we never know when that moment is going to be, doesn't it make sense to decide right now where your ultimate loyalty lies? I know, we all believe that nothing will happen to us until we are ninety-two years old and then one night, we will die in our sleep. It is not going to happen that way—not for most of us. Death and tragedy are no respecters of age. I encourage you to decide, before you finish this chapter, where your ultimate loyalty lies.

Second, worship is a gift because worship helps us focus on God's commitment to us more than our commitment to Him.

The book *One Crowded Hour* is the biography of cameraman Neil Davis. In the book, author Tim Bowden recounts a story told to him by Davis about something that happened in 1964 during a conflict between Malaysia and Indonesia in Borneo.

A group of Gurkhas from Nepal were asked if they would be willing to jump from transport planes into combat against the Indonesians if the need arose. The Gurkhas had the right to turn down the request because they had never been trained as paratroopers. Bowden quotes Davis's account of the story:

70

Now the Gurkhas usually agreed to anything, but on this occasion they provisionally rejected the plan. But the next day, one of their NCOs sought out the British officer who had made the request and said they had discussed the matter further and would be prepared to jump under certain conditions.

"What are they?" asked the British officer.

The Gurkhas told him they would jump if the land was marshy or reasonably soft with no rocky outcrops, because they were inexperienced in falling.

The British officer considered this, and said that the dropping area would almost certainly be over jungle, and there would not be any rocky outcrops, so that seemed all right. Was there anything else? Yes, said the Gurkhas. They wanted the plane to fly as slowly as possible and no more than one hundred feet high. The British officer pointed out the planes always did fly as slowly as possible when dropping troops, but to jump from one hundred feet was impossible, because the parachutes would not open in time from that height.

"Oh," said the Gurkhas, "that's all right, then. We'll jump with parachutes anywhere. You didn't mention parachutes before!" (*One Crowded Hour*, Tim Bowden, Collins Publishers, 1987, pp. 75-76)

Now that is commitment. Worship helps us focus on God's commitment to us, more than our commitment to God. In Genesis 8:20, we read a few words about the very unique commitment of

God to Noah, but it also describes God's commitment to you and me: *"Then Noah built an altar to the LORD and, taking some of all the clean animals and clean birds, he sacrificed burnt offerings on it."*

The Jewish people were very strict about the type of animal they could sacrifice. It could not have a spot. It could not have a blemish. Only certain animals could be used. How was Noah fortunate enough to have that kind of animal on the ark? It was because God provided it for him. In Genesis 7:2, God said, *"Take with you seven of every kind of clean animal, a male and its mate."* Only a clean animal could be used in sacrifice.

God provided the animals a year before Noah even had the need to sacrifice them. God was taking care of Noah even before Noah knew he had a need.

That is the type of commitment God has to you and me, as well. God provided the cross of Jesus Christ before you or I ever sinned. He provided the resurrection before our deaths. He has also provided the power and comfort of the Holy Spirit before we need Him, too. That is one reason we worship, to focus on God's commitment to us more than our commitment to Him.

Third, worship is a gift because worship helps us evaluate and correct the position and condition of our heart.

The word "heart" is a very important word in the Bible, and it is used almost 900 times in all types of contexts. The first two times the word heart is used is in Genesis at the beginning of the story of Noah. In Genesis 6:5–6, we read, *"The Lord saw how great man's wickedness on earth had become, and that every inclination of the thoughts of his heart was only evil all the time. The Lord was grieved that he had made man on the earth, and his heart was filled with pain."*

There is no Scripture in the Bible which shows more clearly that what happens in our hearts directly affects the heart of God. We might have a misunderstanding that the condition of our heart is created by our mind. However, what this passage shows is just the opposite. This passage shows that the condition of our heart stimulates our thoughts, and our thoughts stimulate our actions. Isn't that what Jesus also said, *"No good tree bears bad fruit, nor does a bad tree bear good fruit. Each tree is recognized by its own fruit. People do not pick figs from thorn bushes, or grapes from briers. The good man brings good things out of the good stored up **in his heart**, and the evil man brings evil things out of the evil stored up **in his heart*** (emphasis added). *For out of the overflow of his heart his mouth speaks"* (Luke 6:43–45).

The condition of our heart and the position of our heart are important factors that influence the gift of worship.

One day our children asked me if I could fix the sink in their bathroom because the water was not draining. I thought, "No problem, I can fix that in just a few minutes." I pulled the lever up to close off the drain, filled the sink with water, pushed the lever down— nothing happened. The water stayed in the sink. This was going to be a bigger challenge than I first realized.

No matter what worship style we try, if the condition of our heart does not change, the quality of our worship will not change either.

Then several thoughts entered my mind, What if the sink never drained? It would be okay for one day. It would just fill up with soap, shaving cream and tooth paste. Maybe we could cover it with a towel and pretend it isn't there. Maybe I could polish the faucet and get the kids' attention off the water. After all, we've only lived in this house two years. The previous owners lived here six and a half years.

My thinking got more and more absurd. How often do we have those same thoughts when it comes to the condition of our hearts?

While we can't control what happens to us, we are always in control of how our heart responds.

Things happen in life and we can experience pain, sorrow, hurt, disappointment, rejection, and maybe even abuse. If we hold onto that pain, hurt, sorrow, unforgiveness, bitterness, and anger, then the water of our life gets very unsightly. It does not matter how expensive the marble sink is, how beautiful the monogrammed towel is that you cover it with, or what the faucet looks like. The fact is that the water is still unsightly. Even if our life has a new owner and we have invited Jesus into our life, if we are holding onto pain from the past, the sink is still clogged up.

What happens when we try to worship with a closed heart and a clogged life? It ends up being meaningless and empty. No matter what worship style we try, if the condition of our heart does not change, the quality of our worship will not change either.

The problem with the kids' sink was that the sink stopper had come disconnected from the lever. How it happened, I don't know. When it happened, I don't know. It just happened. I certainly was not trying to blame someone for the condition of the sink. What is sad is that in my own life I spent years trying to blame others for the condition of my heart. Sure, things happen to us that we do not welcome and do not plan. While we can't control what happens to us, however, we are always in control of how our heart responds.

To fix the kids' sink, I reconnected the lever to the sink stopper. When I pushed the lever down, it pushed the sink stopper up. As a result, the dirty water left. Clean, fresh water could flow. The same dynamic happens in worship. When we humble ourselves before God, like pushing the lever down on a sink, our hearts are lifted before God. Then all the stuff that we have been holding onto gets flushed out and the fresh, cleansing love, mercy, and forgiveness of God can cleanse our life.

"Then Noah built an altar to the Lord and, taking some of all the clean animals and clean birds, he sacrificed burnt offerings on it" (Genesis 8:20). Noah humbled himself before God and his heart was lifted up to God in worship. God's heart was pleased, but it wasn't primarily because of the burnt offering. God's heart was pleased because of the condition and position of Noah's heart. What is the position and condition of your heart before God?

Fourth, worship is a gift because worship allows us to yield our whole life to God.

There is a passage in Matthew 3 describing Jesus' baptism. It helps us understand this concept more clearly: *"Then Jesus came from Galilee to the Jordan to be baptized by John. But John tried to deter him saying, 'I need to be baptized by you, and do you come to me?' Jesus replied, 'Let it be so now; it is proper for us to do this to fulfill all righteousness.' Then John consented"* (Matthew 3:13–15).

The last word used in that passage is a very important word. In the NIV it is translated as "consented." In Greek the word is *aphiemi* (af-ee`-ay-mee). The word means to yield, to totally yield yourself to another. John the Baptist yielded himself to Jesus Christ. It was a decision of the heart and the mind. It was a conscious decision to yield everything that was his, all of his being, his whole life to Jesus Christ. He placed himself under the Lordship of Jesus. He placed himself under the authority of Jesus. He placed himself under the control of Jesus. He pledged his total allegiance to Jesus.

Shouldn't we be challenged to broaden our concept of worship from an event to a lifestyle?

That is what worship is all about. In worship we "aphiemi" ourselves to Jesus. By a conscious decision of our mind, we yield to the Lordship of Jesus, to the authority of Jesus, and to the control of Jesus in every area of our life. Anything less is not true worship.

In Noah's life, he was a man who yielded to God as a way of life. In Genesis 6:9, we read this description of Noah: *"[H]e walked with God."* Worship for Noah was not an event for one day of the week; it was a way of life—constantly yielding to the authority and control of God as a way of life. Shouldn't we be challenged to do the same? Shouldn't we be challenged to broaden our concept of worship from an event to a lifestyle?

Another passage in the Old Testament that helps us understand this concept is the story of Shadrach, Meshach and Abednego in Daniel 3. If you are not familiar with this story, I encourage you to read Daniel 1–3.

King Nebuchadnezzar made a golden image and forced everyone to bow down to the image: *"Then the herald loudly proclaimed, 'This is what you are commanded to do, O peoples, nations and men of every language: As soon as you hear the sound of the horn, flute, zither, lyre, harp, pipes and all kinds of music, you must fall down and* **worship** *the image of gold that King Nebuchadnezzar has set up. Whoever does not fall down and* **worship** *will immediately be thrown into a blazing furnace"* (Daniel 3:4–6; emphasis added).

The word "worship" used here in Daniel 3 is the word *seg-eed*. It means to lie prostrate across the floor with your face down to the ground. It symbolizes the same concept as "aphiemi" in Matthew 3. It means to yield totally to the lordship and authority of the other person.

That is what King Nebuchadnezzar asked all people to do. There just happened to be three young Jewish men who said no. Furious with rage, King Nebuchadnezzar summoned Shadrach, Meshach, and Abednego. These men were brought before the king. King Nebuchadnezzar said to them that if they were not willing to bow down and worship and be prostrate in front of the image, they were going to be thrown into the fiery furnace: *"Shadrach, Meshach and Abednego replied to the king, 'O Nebuchadnezzar, we do not need to defend ourselves before you in this matter. If we are thrown into the blazing furnace, the God we serve is able to save us from it, and he will rescue us from your hand, O king.* **But even if he does not**, *we want you to know, O king, that we will not serve your gods or worship the image of gold you have set up"'* (Daniel 3:16–18; emphasis added). I encourage you to read the rest of the story.

The six words "**but even if he does not**," are some of the most important words in the entire Bible. These men said that no matter what happened, they would only worship the one true God. They said that no matter how hot the fiery furnace got, no matter what the king did to them physically, no matter what happened, they still chose to worship the one true God and Him alone.

I wonder how many of us have made the same decision. I challenge you to do that. Making that decision will add a new dimension in worship that you will never want to be without. It is a decision that no matter what happens to you, your family, your job, your car, your finances, your relationships, or anything else, you will still choose to worship the one true God and Him alone.

Noah had obviously made that decision. How do we know that? Because after everything was washed away, when he came out of the ark, the first thing he did was worship. Worship would not have been on his mind and heart if they had been void while he was in the ark. It seems that human behavior causes people to run to God in the midst of problems and then turn away when the problems are over. If that had been true for Noah, he might have worshipped in the ark, but not afterwards.

Worship is a gift we can't afford to lose because worship allows us to yield our whole life to God.

The two weeks after I worked on Diana's greenhouse, I went to Mexico and attended the Spanish Institute of Puebla. Our daughter, Trisha, was in Puebla for a month. My wife, Diana, was with her the first two weeks, and I was with her the last two weeks. The institute is a total-immersion program. There you lived with a family, attended class, had a guide to tour the city in the afternoon, and then studied at night. It was an intense and enjoyable two weeks.

One afternoon my guide, Juan, took me to visit a former convent that had been converted into a museum. It is called the Exconvento de Santa Maria and was built in the 1560s. As Juan took me through that ancient and holy place, I could sense the presence of God. Juan talked about the nuns and their sacrifice, discipline, lifestyle, and mission. We came to one of the bedrooms where I saw a wood bed with no mattress and a wood pillow. I also saw a small room where the nuns were buried. As we walked through the rest of the buildings, Juan told me story after story. I

> *Worship is a gift we can't afford to lose because worship allows us to yield our whole life to God.*

was awed and humbled. Especially when he told me that it had been a convent for four hundred years. This convent was not built by accident, and the nuns did not sacrifice and discipline themselves generation after generation without a reason. The building stands today as a vivid testimony of generations of people who totally yielded their entire lives to God.

We do not have to live in a convent to totally yield our life to God. John the Baptist didn't. Shadrach, Meshach, and Abednego didn't. It is not where we live but how we live that matters. Worship is a gift we can't afford to lose because worship allows us to yield our whole life to God.

Questions

■ What did you learn from the story about Pike's Peak?

■ In what ways can worship teach us that our highest loyalty is to the eternal, not the temporal?

■ What keeps us from fully grasping that truth?

■ How does worship help us focus on God's commit-ment to us, more than our commitment to God?

■ What would Noah suggest regarding our views about worship?

6

Gift Six

Covenant

*Then God blessed Noah and his sons, saying to them, "Be
fruitful and increase in number and fill the earth. The fear
and dread of you will fall upon all the beasts of the earth
and all the birds of the air, upon every creature that moves
along the ground, and upon all the fish of the sea; they are
given into your hands. Everything that lives and moves will
be food for you. Just as I gave you the green plants, I now give
you everything.*

*"But you must not eat meat that has its lifeblood still in it.
And for your lifeblood I will surely demand an accounting.
I will demand an accounting from every animal. And from
each man, too, I will demand an accounting for the life of
his fellow man.*

"Whoever sheds the blood of man, by man shall his blood be shed; for in the image of God, has God made man.

"As for you, be fruitful and increase in number; multiply on the earth and increase upon it."

Then God said to Noah and to his sons with him: "I now establish my covenant with you and with your descendants after you and with every living creature that was with you— the birds, the livestock and all the wild animals, all those that came out of the ark with you—every living creature on earth. I establish my covenant with you: Never again will all life be cut off by the waters of a flood; never again will there be a flood to destroy the earth."

And God said, "This is the sign of the covenant I am making between me and you and every living creature with you, a covenant for all generations to come: I have set my rainbow in the clouds, and it will be the sign of the covenant between me and the earth. Whenever I bring clouds over the earth and the rainbow appears in the clouds, I will remember my covenant between me and you and all living creatures of every kind. Never again will the waters become a flood to destroy all life. Whenever the rainbow appears in the clouds, I will see it and remember the everlasting covenant between God and all living creatures of every kind on the earth."

So God said to Noah, "This is the sign of the covenant I have established between me and all life on the earth."

—Genesis 9:1–17

Many years ago I developed a habit that has been very good for my work. Every summer for about five or six days, I go off by myself for study and prayer. My wife, Diana, and our two children, Matt and Trisha, know that sometime during the summer, Dad will be gone for five or six days. Many summers ago, as I was getting ready, our daughter, Trisha—who was seven—had a difficult time with me being gone. On a Sunday afternoon, I packed everything I was going to take and did not notice that Trisha had gone into her room. She was very quiet. Just about the time I finished packing, she came into our bedroom, sat on the bed, and said, "Daddy?" I said, "Yeah, Trish." I sat beside her and put my arm around her. She said, "How long are you going to be gone?" I picked her up, put her in my lap, hugged her, and said, "About five or six days. Why? Are you going to miss me?" A tear came to her eye and she nodded her head. I didn't notice until then that she had something clutched in her hand. She put her hand out and her fingers began to unbend.

She said, "Daddy, on your trip I want you to take this." In her hand was a locket. She opened the locket and inside was a picture of our family. She said, "Daddy, when I was in kindergarten, some days I really missed you and Mommy and Bubba. Mommy gave me this locket to take to school so whenever I got really lonely, I would open it up and look at our family and I would feel a lot better. I want you to take it on your trip this week so that when you get lonely, you can open it up, and you can feel better." Well, you talk about tears! She was crying, I was crying, and we were hugging each other. What was so exciting about that moment was not just the gift of the locket, but the fact that a seven-year-old girl had already learned that love is giving yourself away so that someone else will receive a blessing.

A binding agreement made during a moment of strength, so that during a moment of weakness it will not be unbound.

This chapter focuses on covenant, because the covenant we have with God is a gift we can't afford to lose. When we look at the entire story of Noah in Genesis 6–9—we see that this story is a story of covenant. From beginning to end, this story is about the covenant between God, Noah, and Noah's family. It is really more than a covenant between God and Noah. It is also a covenant between God and the entire human race.

A definition of covenant is this: a binding agreement made during a moment of strength, so that during a moment of weakness it will not be unbound. During the story of Noah in Genesis, and throughout the entire Bible, it is always God's strength and our weakness.

Let me summarize the story up to this point. God gave Noah the vision to build the ark. One hundred years later, when the ark was complete, God gathered the animals and they joined Noah and his family in the ark. Including the forty days of rain, the inhabitants stayed in the ark 375 days. Then when God called Noah out of the ark, the first thing he did was to build an altar and worship God. After that worship experience was over, Noah was ready to start a new chapter in his life.

God spoke to Noah in a very powerful way and said, *"I now establish my covenant with you and with your descendants after you"* (Genesis 9:9).

What God shared with Noah at that moment and what Noah experienced in that encounter with God provide three reasons why the covenant between God and humankind is a gift we can't afford to lose.

First, the covenant between God and humankind is a gift because it is a God-initiated covenant.

Prior to the ark being built, God spoke about this covenant that was going to be established in the future. In Genesis 6:18, just after God spoke about the flood and the destruction of life on earth, He said to Noah, *"**But I will** establish my covenant with you"* (emphasis added). After the flood, God spoke about the covenant again. However, instead of speaking about the covenant in the future, the time for the covenant was now. Instead of speaking about the covenant once, God spoke about it many times. In addition, God repeatedly spoke as the One who took the responsibility to initiate this covenant. Look at the following list of verses in Genesis that talk about this covenant:

Covenant Words

6:18   *"**I will establish** my covenant with you…"*

9:9   *"**I now establish** my covenant with you…"*

9:11   *"**I establish** my covenant with you…"*

9:12   *"This is the sign of the covenant **I am making** between me and you…"*

9:13   *"…it will be the sign of the covenant **between me and the earth**."*

9:15   *"**I will remember my covenant** between me and you and all living creatures of every kind."*

9:16   *"…I will see it and **remember the everlasting covenant between God and all living creatures** of every kind on the earth."*

9:17   *"…This is the sign of the covenant **I have established** between me and all life on the earth."*

Years ago I heard a powerful story that illustrates this principle. A police officer was taking the place of another police officer who was sick. Because this officer had not been to this particular part of town for a long time and did not know the area well, he decided that during the first hour of his shift he would drive around to reacquaint himself with the area. Immediately after doing this, he received a call on the radio that a child was choking. He knew where the subdivision was and he knew the long way to get there, but he also remembered that the city had just built a new part of the freeway. He was not too far from the entrance to the freeway, so he got on the freeway, sped about four miles and got to the place where he was to exit. Panic struck his face when he realized that the exit ramp had not yet been built. He slammed on his brakes, got out of the car and looked over to the side of the freeway that was basically like a cliff. He did not know what to do. It was four miles back to the off-ramp. Then he would have to go all through the subdivision, and he knew if he took all that time, the child would not make it.

He was trying to figure out what to do when all of a sudden he heard a loud noise behind him. He turned around and there was a huge bulldozer with a man sitting on top. The bulldozer operator said, "Officer, what can I do for you?" The officer explained about the child who was choking and not being able to get to him. The bulldozer operator said, "No problem, just follow me." The bulldozer literally carved a road in the side of that hill and the police officer went down the hill right behind the bulldozer. At the bottom of the hill, the bulldozer went one way and the police car went the other way. The officer found the house, went in, got the baby who was blue by then, turned the baby upside down, and patted him on the back. A marble popped out of the baby's mouth. The baby started breathing on his own and a few minutes later the ambulance came and gave the baby oxygen. The next day, the police officer found the bulldozer operator to personally thank him for his help the day before. The officer got out of his car and the operator walked toward him. When they met, the officer began by saying, "I just want to thank you for what you did yesterday." The operator said, "No, I want to thank you." The officer said, "Why do you want to thank me?" The operator said, "You don't understand; that baby was my own son."

A life was spared because someone was willing to carve a path where there was no path and to make a way where there was no way. God did the same thing during the days of Noah. Before God spoke to Noah about the covenant in Genesis 9, we read these words in Genesis 8:21, *"The Lord smelled the pleasing aroma and said in his heart: 'Never again will I curse the ground because of man,* ***even though every inclination of his heart is evil from childhood'"*** (emphasis added).

God knew that even though the human race was beginning again with Noah's family, the inner character of humankind would not change. Yet God was still willing to initiate and establish a covenant with Noah and all future generations.

God did the same thing for you and me through His Son, Jesus Christ. God initiated the New Covenant through His Son, Jesus. Jesus came into this earth and carved a path where there was no path and made a way where there was no way. In Romans 5:8, we read these words, *"But God demonstrates his own love for us in this: While we were still sinners, Christ died for us."* That all happened because Jesus Christ came into our world at the point of our need. He made a way through human sin when there was no way; He carved a path where there was no path. This God-initiated covenant with Jesus Christ shows that God is willing to make a commitment to us before He ever asks for a commitment from us.

Second, this covenant between God and humankind is a gift but we must receive it.

During the presidency of Andrew Jackson, a man by the name of George Wilson robbed a mail train, during which he wounded a mail carrier. He was brought to trial, found guilty, and was given the death penalty. However, President Jackson granted Wilson a pardon; but Wilson refused it. There was such controversy over the fact that he had refused a presidential pardon that the case went to the U.S. Supreme Court. The Supreme Court argued his case. It was during that time that Chief Justice John Marshall was on the bench. Marshall wrote these words:

> A pardon is an act of grace, proceeding from the power entrusted with the execution of the laws, which exempts the individual, on whom it is bestowed, from the punishment the law inflicts for a crime he has committed...

A pardon is a deed, to the validity of which delivery is essential; and delivery is not completed without acceptance. It may then be rejected by the person to whom it is tendered; and if it be rejected, we have discovered no power in a court to force it on him.

It may be supposed that no being condemned to death would reject a pardon, but the rule must be the same in capital cases and in misdemeanors. (https://supreme. justia.com/federal/us/32/150/case.html)

In other words, George Wilson committed a crime. He was tried and found guilty. He was sentenced to be executed. A presidential decree granted him a full pardon. But George Wilson chose rather to refuse that pardon. The courts concluded that the pardon could not be forced upon him.

This God-initiated covenant is a gift God offers to us. It is a binding agreement between God and us, but only if we accept it! This covenant is not something He forces on us. It is something God offers as a gift, so it is only effective in our life if we receive it.

God said, *"I have set my rainbow in the clouds, and it will be the sign of the covenant between me and the earth. Whenever I bring clouds over the earth and the rainbow appears in the clouds, I will remember my covenant between me and you and all living creatures of every kind"* (Genesis 9:13–15). We still have the rainbow in the clouds as a visible reminder of God's covenant between us and Him. However, even more importantly for you and me today, we also have the cross of Jesus Christ. The cross is there to remind us that the covenant was not only offered but it must be received.

Third, this covenant between God and humankind is a gift because the covenant is eternal. The Vietnam War has many painful memories for many people. One of the few good memories to come out of the war was written about in the February 13, 1987 issue of *The Missileer*, a newspaper published for the Eastern Space and Missile Center at Patrick Air Force Base in Florida. In an article written by Center commander Colonel John W. Mansur, he recounted a story someone told him that he was not sure how much, if any, was true. Nonetheless, Mansur felt the need to share the touching story in *The Missileer*. The story goes like this:

Mortar rounds struck an orphanage in a small village. People from the village came around to see what was happening. Someone was sent to the next village where an American Navy doctor and nurse were stationed. Several minutes later, the doctor and nurse came to the orphanage. An eight-year-old girl was the most severely wounded. They immediately determined that if she did not receive a blood transfusion, she would die. The doctor and nurse typed her blood and realized that neither of them had the same blood type. The doctor spoke broken Vietnamese, and the nurse spoke broken high school French. They asked, as best they could, which of the children would volunteer to give blood for their friend. All the children's eyes got big, but no one volunteered.

Finally, one little hand went up, shaking, and the nurse went over to the boy and asked his name. He said his name was Heng. She picked him up and put him on a bed right next to the girl. The nurse rubbed his arm with alcohol and stuck a needle in, and when she did, the boy started to weep. He wept so loudly, he stuck his fist in his mouth so he would not cry. But he kept crying, louder and louder. The doctor and nurse thought they had hurt him. He continued to weep with his fist in his mouth. Finally, a Vietnamese nurse arrived. They communicated their concern for the young boy. She went over and began to talk with the boy. Soon, he stopped crying and wiped his face and began to smile. The Vietnamese nurse explained to the American doctor and nurse that when the boy was asked to give blood, he thought he had to give all of his blood in order for his friend to live.

In John 15:13, we read these words, *"Greater love has no one than this, that he lay down his life for his friends."* That is exactly what Jesus did for you and for me. He gave all his blood so you and I could be set free. It's a God-initiated covenant. It's a covenant that must be received. It is also a covenant that is eternal. In Genesis 9:16, we read these words, *"Whenever the rainbow appears in the clouds, I will see it and remember the everlasting covenant between God and all living creatures."* We still have the rainbow, but the sign of the covenant that is even more powerful for you and for me is the sign of the cross. Jesus came and carved a way where there was no way; He carved a path where there was no path because He wants us to accept this covenant now and experience the joy of it for eternity.

Several years ago I received a letter from a young man who I will call Thomas Long, which is not his actual name. Thomas was a member of the church where I was the pastor. He was there for about a year and all of a sudden, one day, he was gone. I received a letter from him; he was writing from jail in Colorado. I would like to quote the letter here word for word:

Hello Church Members. Some of you will remember me and some of you will not. I was the young man that joined the church about this time last year. Some of you know that I had just gotten out of drug rehab and I had joined the church looking for spiritual help. Well, it would have helped me but I didn't understand religion and faith. I thought it was just a lot of singing and talking to God. So I became frustrated and went back to drugs, looking for an escape from life. All I found was jail. And now I am facing time here in Colorado and in Texas. I've been here in jail almost five months now. When I was put here I prayed something would change and that I wouldn't have the urge for drugs anymore. For they were destroying my life. Well, almost two months ago, I met a friend named Keith. He gave me a Bible and taught me what faith is all about and I haven't been the same since. I read my Bible every night and study it too. It's like a miracle. I was down this far and God still heard me. He is truly a loving and forgiving God and He and His Son, Jesus will help anyone who calls out to them. I thought it would be nice to share my miracle with all of you. Maybe if there is

Wherever you are in your life right now and no matter how long you have been there, God wants to make a way where there is no way. He wants to carve a path into your life where you believe there is no path. He wants to come to you at the point of your greatest need, reach down with the saving power of the cross, and lift you up and make you whole.

someone out there with lack of faith, this letter will give them hope. Well, I want to tell you it might be a while before I return to church, but don't take me off the membership list just yet. Because someday when you least expect it, I will come walking back through that door with Bible in hand. That is my promise to you and to God. I would like to hear from some of you if at all possible. Please by all means, if you have anything of knowledge or a good Scripture to read, I would greatly appreciate it. I love and think of all of you all the time. Love, Thomas Long. P.S. If you believe you will receive whatever you ask for in prayer.

Most people do not live in the county jail. However, my experience has taught me that sometimes the invisible bars of sin, shame, guilt, bitterness, hatred, criticism, enmity, and meanness are more confining than the bars of the county jail. Wherever you are in your life right now and no matter how long you have been there, God wants to make a way where there is no way. He wants to carve a path into your life where you believe there is no path. He wants to come to you at the point of your greatest need, reach down with the saving power of the cross, and lift you up and make you whole. It is all about the covenant. The covenant is a gift we can't afford to lose because it is God-initiated. It will change our life when we accept it. This covenant also can begin now and last for all eternity.

Diana and I were married in 1977. For our honeymoon, we went to Fort Myers Beach, Florida. We toured Fort Myers Beach and went to Thomas Edison's winter home, which was a fabulous experience. Many years later we took our children back to Fort Myers and to Sanibel Island. Sanibel Island is the shelling capitol of the United States. We spent a week in the water, collecting seashells. We still have boxes of them in the garage. One day we went to see the Thomas Edison home. Right next door was the Henry Ford winter home. When we went in 1977, the city of Fort Myers did not own that home. However, since that time, the city purchased the Ford home. When we were going through those homes, our tour guide told us a fascinating story that happened between Mrs. Mina Miller Edison and Henry Ford.

Thomas Edison was a workaholic. He spent all of his time in his laboratory. Mrs. Edison took it upon herself to invite friends from all over the United States to spend time with her so she wouldn't be lonely. When anyone accepted her invitation, she asked them to bring a stone with their name carved on it. That would be their gift to Mrs. Edison. She used the stones to make a walkway in her garden. One day she went next door and asked Ford to come over for dinner. She told him when he came to bring a stone with his name carved on it. A couple of weeks later, Ford accepted the invitation. When he came he brought a stone, but there was nothing carved in it. Mrs. Edison turned to the multimillionaire and asked, "Mr. Ford, why is it that you do not have your name carved in it?" He said, "I simply could not afford it." She took the stone and placed it in the ground. If you go there today, you will get to walk along that path with all the stones with names carved in them; there is only one stone with no name. It is the stone from Henry Ford. Ford is remembered around

> *I hope you don't remember this day for something you did not do.*

the world for the many things he did. However, on that one spot, he will be forever remembered for something he did not do.

As you finish this chapter, I hope you don't remember this day for something you did not do. Jesus came to earth to offer His covenant to you. I encourage you to receive it because it is an eternal covenant between you and Jesus that starts now and lasts through all eternity. Truly, this God-initiated covenant is a gift we can't afford to lose.

Questions

- How do you describe the word "covenant?"

- How does it apply to your relationship with God?

- What role did the covenant play in Noah's story?

- How can you let it play a deeper role in your own story?

7

Gift Seven
Prayer

When men began to increase in number on the earth and daughters were born to them, the sons of God saw that the daughters of men were beautiful, and they married any of them they chose. Then the LORD said, "My Spirit will not contend with man forever, for he is mortal; his days will be a hundred and twenty years."

The Nephilim were on the earth in those days—and also afterward—when the sons of God went to the daughters of men and had children by them. They were the heroes of old, men of renown.

The LORD saw how great man's wickedness on the earth had become, and that every inclination of the thoughts of his heart was only evil all the time. The LORD was grieved that he had made man on the earth, and his heart was filled with pain. So the LORD said, "I will wipe mankind, whom I have created, from the face of the earth—men and animals, and creatures that move along the ground, and birds of the air— for I am grieved that I have made them." But Noah found favor in the eyes of the LORD.

This is the account of Noah.

Noah was a righteous man, blameless among the people of his time, and he walked with God.

—Genesis 6:1–9

Several years ago, I went to Larry's Shoes to buy some tennis shoes that would accommodate the ankle brace I now have to wear since I broke my ankle. The shoes I had been wearing were discontinued, so I discussed the situation with a salesman. He did everything he could to find a shoe that would fit. Before long, another salesman came over with some catalogs and all three of us looked at the shoes in the catalogs. All of a sudden a man, probably in his mid-sixties, whom I had never met, came over and introduced himself. He said, "Hi, my name is Larry Goodwin." I said, "Hi, my name is Dean Posey." The salesman told Mr. Goodwin the whole story about my shoe dilemma. Then Mr. Goodwin said, "Well, I tell you what. If you can't find a shoe, I'll call the warehouse and ask them if there is anything there. Even though they don't make that shoe anymore, they could still have it in the warehouse." He then handed me his card and said, "Just let me know." I said, "Thank you very much," and then he was gone. I looked down at his card: Larry Goodwin, chairman of the board. I had just met Larry from Larry's Shoes, and I did not even know it until he was gone.

God is the ultimate chairman of the board. We read in the Bible that God is willing to do more for us than we ever ask or think. He is willing to meet our needs before we even know we have a need or ask for it to be filled. In addition, we have the opportunity, at any time, through prayer, to talk to the ultimate chairman of the board.

What is interesting about the story of Noah and the ark is that the word "prayer" is not found in the story at all. However, when we have a healthy understanding of prayer, we will come to the conclusion that Noah had to be a praying man because of how he related to God and how God related to him. We can look at the story of Noah and ask: What can this story teach me about prayer? We can learn three important lessons about prayer and learn why prayer is a gift we can't afford to lose.

First, prayer is a gift because it is through prayer that we develop and maintain our intimacy with God.

"Noah was a righteous man, blameless among the people of his time, and he walked with God" (Genesis 6:9). Those four words, *"he walked with God,"* mean that he had a daily relationship with God. Those four words are a statement about his life, character, integrity, habits, and priorities. I can think of few compliments that are greater than to be known as a person who walks with God.

Our son, Matt, gave me a T-shirt once with this message printed on it: "You can talk the talk, but can you walk the walk?"

Noah was obviously a person who had a reputation of walking the walk. I wonder how many of us today have a desire to be a person who has the reputation of walking with God. It is so easy to work toward a reputation that is different than Noah's. Many people have a desire for a reputation in their work, their financial status, or their service to the community. There is nothing wrong with working toward that type of reputation. After all, Noah also had a reputation as a great ship builder and zookeeper.

However, from the very beginning, this story of Noah challenges us to examine the primary reputation of our life.

Do you want to be a person who walks with God? It is important to notice that Noah did not say this about himself. Someone else said this about him. Before you begin working toward that goal, I suggest that you do it humbly and cautiously. If you don't, you will quickly gain a reputation that is opposite of what you desire.

To begin walking with God, we need a personal relationship with God, through His Son, Jesus. This relationship is possible, but not because we initiate it. This relationship is possible because God initiates the relationship with us and gives us the gift of faith to believe in Him.

My wife, Diana, and I enjoy eating popcorn. We normally eat it three or four times a week. We have eaten many different varieties and flavors. When our children were small, we ate popcorn after we had put them to bed. "Popcorn time" became for us an intimate time of talking, dreaming, and sharing our joys and concerns. Many times our popcorn time was the highlight of our day because we both knew we could talk about anything and be with someone who loved us, accepted us, and supported us.

If we are learning to walk with God, we need to make popcorn time with Jesus a priority in our life. Not that we actually eat popcorn, but we have the time alone with Jesus, to share our heart and to listen to His.

Many people today are searching for acceptance. It is amazing what some people will do to be accepted by others. We will never experience acceptance of our actions if we don't first experience acceptance of our "being." Spending time alone with Jesus allows us to be with the One who accepts us right where we are and just the way we are. The more time we spend alone with Jesus, the more we develop and maintain our intimacy with Him. The main purpose of prayer is not so we can hear what Jesus wants us to do. Rather, it is so we can more clearly discover who He is. Only after we discover who He is, will we discover who He wants us to be and what He wants us to do. It is through these times of intimacy that Jesus can influence our view of Himself in addition to our life, character, integrity, habits, and priorities. Time with Jesus is when we learn to walk with God.

Second, prayer is a gift because it is through prayer that we learn to recognize the voice of God.

Several years ago I decided to give my children an education in life. I took them to a junk yard. I needed a part for the emergency brake system for my truck and I figured it could be found in a junkyard. So we went looking.

As we arrived and got out of the car, the kids began asking questions about where we were and what we were going to do. They were fascinated by all the things they saw that they had never seen before. They asked questions about why one car was wrecked and why another one was turned upside down. They were fascinated in the midst of a pile of junk. Trisha said, "Let's get a present for Mom." The first thing that went through my mind was how I could grant her request without making myself look like an idiot. Was Trisha thinking about getting her a hubcap or a steering wheel? Finally I said, "What about a rock? Let's take a rock to Mom." That was enough to satisfy her need to give a gift to her parent.

What is amazing is that in the midst of a place she had never been and in the midst of a place that had more things than she could possibly imagine taking home, she didn't ask for a present for herself. Rather, she asked for a present for her mother. Her focus was not on getting something; rather it was on giving something. Her focus was not upon herself; her focus was on her parent.

We live in a world that is many times filled with broken lives and broken dreams— not just broken cars. We live in a world that is filled with disappointment and frustration instead of pots of gold at the end of the rainbow. As a result, when we pray it is easy to focus upon God hearing our voice instead of us hearing His. It is easy to ask God to do what we want instead of listening quietly for His voice. It is easy for prayer to become focused on getting instead of giving and focused upon ourselves instead of God.

Think for a moment what would have happened between God and Noah if Noah had been focused on his own needs in prayer instead of on hearing the voice of God. How many times would God have had to speak in order for Noah to hear, if he heard at all? How many times would God have had to speak the vision before Noah would have comprehended what was being said? All of us who live after Noah can be thankful that God only had to speak once, and Noah heard.

It is not easy to develop a prayer life like Noah, but it is possible. For Noah, his prayer life was not complete without the obedience that followed. After God spoke of the ark, *"Noah did everything just as God commanded him"* (Genesis 6:22). God spoke again after the ark was complete and told Noah about the animals, *"And Noah did all that the Lord commanded him"* (Genesis 7:5).

For Noah, prayer was not complete until obedience was complete. Prayer was like breathing; Noah breathed in the voice of God, and he breathed out obedience. For Noah, the two were inseparable. I believe God thinks the same way.

The more we listen, the more we recognize the voice of God. We learn to distinguish His voice from our own voice. The more obedient we are to His voice, the more He can trust us with a bigger and bigger vision.

All of us who live after Noah can be thankful that he prayed enough to recognize the voice of God and that he was obedient to the One whom he heard.

Third, prayer is a gift because it is through prayer that we grow in our confidence in God.

In Genesis 6:13, *"...God said to Noah..."* That is the first recorded conversation between God and a person since God spoke to Cain (Genesis 4:15), which was approximately 1,400 years earlier. See **Chart 2: Generations from Adam to Noah** (on the next page). God could have spoken to people between Cain and Noah; it is just not recorded in the Bible.

Chart 2
Generations from Adam to Noah
(Genesis 5:3-32)

Adam's son Seth was born when Adam was 130. Adam lived an additional 800 years for a total of 930 years.

Seth's son Enosh was born when Seth was 105. Seth lived an additional 807 years for a total of 912 years.

Enosh's son Kenan was born when Enosh was 90. Enosh lived an additional 815 years for a total of 905 years.

Kenan's son Mahalalel was born when Kenan was 70. Kenan lived an additional 840 years for a total of 910 years.

Mahalalel's son Jared was born when Mahalalel was 65. Mahalalel lived an additional 830 years for a total of 895 years.

Jared's son Enoch was born when Jared was 162. Jared lived an additional 800 years for a total of 962 years.

Enoch's son Methuselah was born when Enoch was 65. Enoch lived an additional 300 years for a total of 365 years.

Methuselah's son Lamech was born when Methuselah was 187. Methuselah lived an additional 782 years for a total of 969 years.

Lamech's son Noah was born when Lamech was 182. Lamech lived an additional 595 years for a total of 777 years.

Noah's son Shem was born after Noah was 500. Noah lived an additional 450 years for a total of 950 years.

Even though Adam was 130 years old when Seth was born (Genesis 5:3), God obviously spoke to Cain (Genesis 4:15) prior to Seth's birth. So the number of years between when God spoke to Cain and when He spoke to Noah (Genesis 6:13) was approximately 1400 years.

When God spoke to Noah in Genesis 6:13, He gave Noah the final vision for his life. I say final vision because God does not give us a big vision unless we have been obedient to a small one. It is the same principle Jesus spoke of in the parable of the talents in Matthew 25. To the servant who hid the money in the ground, the master said, *"Take the talent from him and give it to the one who has the ten talents.* **For everyone who has will be given more, and he will have in abundance. Whoever does not have, even what he has will be taken from him"** (Matthew 25:28–29, emphasis added).

Since Noah *"walked with God"* (Genesis 6:9) he had proven his obedience to smaller visions. It was through his obedience to smaller visions that Noah grew in his confidence of hearing the voice of God, and God in His confidence of Noah's obedience. So when God gave Noah the vision of the ark and placed the future of the human race in the hands of Noah, God had no doubt that Noah would be obedient because Noah had been obedient before.

Noah's walk with God was so intimate that God only had to speak the vision once and He knew Noah would be obedient. In addition, after God spoke the vision of the ark, He did not speak to Noah again for one hundred years, until the ark was complete.

It takes a powerful prayer life to have that much confidence in God so when He speaks and gives a vision as big as the ark, we will be obedient even when He is silent. You and I can have that kind of prayer life but it comes with a high price.

Those of us who live in Texas know the significance of March 6, 1836. That was the day of the famous Battle of the Alamo. One of the most significant legends of the Alamo is what Colonel William

Travis did prior to the final battle. He drew a line in the sand and asked his men to join in the battle. As every man stepped across the line, he signed his own death warrant because all of those men died the following day. However, their willingness to sacrifice inspired others to fight. Soon, Texas won its independence from Mexico.

What are we willing to sacrifice? What price are we willing to pay in order to have a prayer life like Noah?

It is a prayer life that has so much confidence in God that when He speaks, we are unquestionably obedient.

Questions

- How does the story about Larry's Shoes relate to this chapter's theme of prayer?

- What biblical stories come to your mind when you read the word "prayer?"

- What personal stories come to your mind when you read the word prayer?

- How did prayer relate to Noah's life?

- How does it relate to your life?

- How could it in the future?

Gift Eight

Friendship

When men began to increase in number on the earth and daughters were born to them, the sons of God saw that the daughters of men were beautiful, and they married any of them they chose. Then the LORD said, "My Spirit will not contend with man forever, for he is mortal; his days will be a hundred and twenty years."

The Nephilim were on the earth in those days—and also afterward—when the sons of God went to the daughters of men and had children by them. They were the heroes of old, men of renown.

The LORD saw how great man's wickedness on the earth had become, and that every inclination of the thoughts of his heart was only evil all the time. The LORD was grieved that *he had made man on the earth, and his heart was filled with pain. So the LORD said, "I will wipe mankind, whom I have created, from the face of the earth—men and animals, and creatures that move along the ground, and birds of the air— for I am grieved that I have made them." But Noah found favor in the eyes of the LORD.*

This is the account of Noah.

Noah was a righteous man, blameless among the people of his time, and he walked with God.

—Genesis 6:1– 9

In August 1973, I was a freshman at Baylor University. On a Monday, I drove from Albuquerque, New Mexico, to Waco, Texas. On Tuesday, I registered for class and fought the line at the bookstore. That night, one of the guys in the dorm asked if I wanted to go with him to the Baptist Student Union. I don't remember our real motivation for going (probably to meet some freshmen girls), but it was a night that changed my life forever.

As several of us were sitting on the floor in the middle of the room, a freshman girl stood at the doorway. I did not really see the guy she was with. But I saw her. She was the most beautiful girl I had ever seen. I turned to the guy sitting next to me and said, "Someday I'm going to have a date with her."

Even though the date did not officially happen for three years, my friendship with Diana began that night. At first we just talked. I took her to church because she had no car. She would call me about boyfriend problems. I would talk to her about girlfriend problems.

Near the end of our junior year, we both attended a retreat at the beach. Even though she came with her boyfriend, we still managed to have a long walk on the beach. During our walk, she updated me on her plans of leaving Baylor to attend a physical therapy school near her home in Memphis, Tennessee. Even though that walk lasted a long time, it seemed to pass in an instant once I realized I might not see her again.

Several weeks later I unexpectedly got a call from Diana. She and her boyfriend had broken up. He was supposed to have helped her move home and then go to Fort Worth, Texas, and attend a Christian conference with her. She asked if I would help her move and then go with her to the conference. I said yes.

As we drove to Memphis she asked me if I was dating anyone. I said no. Then she went through a list of female friends and asked why I didn't date any of them. I remember saying these words, "They are just like you. They are too good of friends to date."

We moved her back to Memphis, then went to the conference in Fort Worth and stayed with my aunt and uncle. Every night after the meeting we sat in the living room and talked for hours. At the end of the week when the conference was over, Diana drove herself back to Memphis. As she drove out of sight, part of my heart went with her because I felt my best friend was leaving and I would never see her again.

Several months later, I called Diana to see if I could come to see her in Memphis before we both started school. She said yes. The day

I got to Memphis, Diana had the flu and was sick for three days. It just so happened that during those three days all the tomatoes in her father's garden ripened. We still laugh about my spending three days helping him can tomatoes.

When Diana got better we went to the Memphis Zoo. We call it our first date because it was the first time we held hands. Whether I reached out and took her hand or she reached out and took mine is still debated in our family.

We were married sixteen months later, one week after she finished physical therapy school. Our experience from friendship, to dating, to marriage has significantly influenced how I approach pre-marriage counseling with couples. In the pre-marriage counseling sessions, I ask many questions and we talk about a variety of subjects. In all the questioning I want to know if it is a marriage between two people or a marriage between best friends.

Not everyone gets married and not everyone has a best friend. However, God has a desire to be everyone's best friend because friendship with God is a gift we can't afford to lose. It is in friendship that we can be ourselves and the other person can be themselves. It is in friendship that we can commit ourselves totally to the other person. It is also in friendship that we are totally dedicated to the well-being of the other.

First, a friendship with God is a gift because a friendship is a relationship in which both people can be themselves.

I don't know if any of us can fully comprehend the depth of the words from Genesis 6:6, 8–9, 13: *"The Lord was grieved that he had made man on the earth, and his heart was filled with pain….But*

Noah found favor in the eyes of the Lord....Noah was a righteous man, blameless among the people of his time, and he walked with God....So God said to Noah..." Yes, Noah had faith in God and he had a deep prayer life. However, these verses tell us that God's heart was filled with pain and He turned to Noah as a man would turn to a friend. In deep friendships, people can be themselves. The closer we get to God, the more we will have the courage to pray, "Father, break my heart with the things that break your heart."

I believe God and Noah had that type of deep friendship. It wasn't just God's heart that was broken and filled with pain about the condition of the world. Noah's heart was broken as well. This type of friendship was also experienced between God and Moses: *"The Lord would speak to Moses face to face, as a man speaks with his friend"* (Exodus 33:11).

Part of the time I was in seminary, I worked at Grady Memorial Hospital as a chaplain intern. My supervisor was Fred Hall. At first, Fred was on my back about everything. Several months later, he helped me understand that my main problem was me. I took a major step toward maturity when I stopped blaming others for my anger, bitterness, and resentment. As Fred helped me be honest with myself and God, God began to bring healing in my life. Before then, I thought I could hide all those hurts from God. Fred helped me realize that as I acknowledged who, what, and how I am before God, then God's peace and tranquility can calm my restlessness.

> *Acknowledging who we are is not a sign of weakness. It is a sign that we have received one of the greatest gifts of all—the gift of a friend.*

That discovery helped me experience the beginning of a friendship with God because I learned I could be myself with Him.

We often try, as I did, to be someone we are not. One of the greatest things we can do for our faith is to be ourselves. As we learn to be ourselves in the presence of God, we will learn over and over again that He accepts us just the way we are. In Psalm 46:10, God says, *"Be still, and know that I am God."* It is easy to look still on the outside; to be still on the inside is the greater challenge. We learn to be still on the inside when we acknowledge before God who and what we are, and accept the fact that we are accepted by Him right where we are and just the way we are.

It is not easy to acknowledge who we really are. Only in the presence of a good friend can we even begin to let our true self show, even to ourselves. Acknowledging who we are is not a sign of weakness. It is a sign that we have received one of the greatest gifts of all—the gift of a friend.

Several years ago my church held a discipleship class in the evening. On the last night of the class, people were encouraged to share what the class had meant to them. One man, who I will call Ted, stood up and said, "Hi, my name is Ted, and I'm an alcoh…. Oh! Sorry, wrong meeting." Even though everyone laughed, including Ted, everyone knew what was happening. Ted had just become a Christian and this was his first discipleship class. He felt so comfortable around the other people, he could be who he was, knowing that everyone accepted him just the way he was. If people will do that with other people, they can be themselves in the presence of God.

Second, a friendship with God is a gift because a friendship is a relationship in which we can commit ourselves totally to the other person.

My favorite movie of all time is *It's a Wonderful Life.* In the beginning of the movie, George Bailey saves the life of his younger brother, Harry. George and his friends are sliding down an icy hill while sitting on a shovel. Harry slides too far and falls into the icy water. The only reason his life is saved is because George jumps in after him. The other boys try to reach him by lying on the ice, but the only one who could save him was the one who was totally committed.

Later in the movie, George stands on a bridge and looks down into the icy river while he thinks about suicide. All of a sudden Clarence, the angel, jumps into the river, and once again George jumps into the icy water to save someone. Clarence later explains to George, "I jumped in to save you, George."

Jumping into warm water to save someone's life takes courage and commitment. How much more commitment does it take to jump into icy water? It takes total commitment.

Genesis 6:5 says, *"The Lord saw how great man's wickedness on earth had become…"* It's as if the icy waters of human sin had covered the earth long before the waters of the flood. The only way humankind could be saved was if God could find someone He could trust and be totally committed to Him and His purposes.

In Psalm 14:2–3 we read, *"The Lord looks down from heaven on the sons of men to see if there are any who understand, any who seek God. All have turned aside, they have together become corrupt; there is no one who does good, not even one."*

At that time, there was, obviously, no one God could turn to as a friend because *"all have turned aside."* However, during Noah's lifetime, God could trust and be totally committed to Noah, and Noah had proven that he trusted and was totally committed to God. When God gave Noah the vision of the ark, Noah completely committed himself to the task.

One of the most significant verses in the Bible that focuses on the commitment of one human being to another is Ruth 1:16, where Ruth said to her mother-in-law, Naomi, *"Where you go I will go, and where you stay I will stay. Your people will be my people and your God my God."* Ruth made a total commitment of herself to Naomi. She made that commitment without realizing how that commitment would influence her own life. When we read the entire book of Ruth, we see that Ruth's total commitment to Naomi, and then to Boaz, not only changed her own life, but also changed human history (since she became the great-grandmother of King David).

Noah's total commitment to God not only changed his life, but his commitment changed human history.

Noah's total commitment to God is stated in Genesis 6:9, *"Noah was a righteous man, blameless among the people of his time, and he walked with God."* In this verse is a reference to Noah's moral character. The word "blameless" refers to his integrity. The word "walked" can also mean to travel. Noah was known as a man of outstanding moral character, with integrity as solid as granite, who traveled through life in complete, unqualified surrender to God. No wonder God could trust him with a vision and a task as big as the ark. Imagine what God could do with others who chose to live the same way.

Two of those people were Enoch and Abraham. In Genesis 5:24, we read, *"Enoch walked with God."* In Genesis 17:1, God said to Abraham, *"I am God Almighty; walk before me and be blameless."*

In all three passages, the word walk is the same Hebrew word, *halak.*

In Leviticus 26:12, God spoke of the relationship He desired to have with the people of Israel and His commitment to it. He said, *"I will walk among you and be your God, and you will be my people."*

It is obvious that the word walk means more than a walk around the block. Rather, it means total commitment to the other person. Noah's total commitment to God not only changed his life, but his commitment changed human history.

There are different levels of friendship between individuals. In my experience, there are at least five levels of friendship:

Level One: Non friend
Level Two: Acquaintance
Level Three: Friend
Level Four: Good friend
Level Five: Best friend

The more someone becomes a friend, it is like peeling the layers off an onion; deeper and deeper levels of friendship are exposed and experienced. It is difficult to commit ourselves totally to the other person at the outer layers of friendship. As a deeper level of friendship is experienced, we become more and more willing to make a bigger commitment of ourselves to the other.

This dynamic is true in our relationship with people and in our relationship with God. In our relationship with God, the more consistently we choose to move from acquaintance to best friend, the more our commitment will move from barely committed to totally committed. It was Noah's total commitment to God that motivated Noah to do *"everything just as God commanded him"* (Genesis 6:22).

When people are in a relationship in which they can commit themselves totally to the other person, they are also dedicated to the well-being of the other. In John 15:13, Jesus said, *"Greater love has no one than this, that he lay down his life for his friends."* Jesus laid down His life, not for His own sake, but for the sake and the well-being of His friends.

Noah also laid down his life. Yes, it was different than Jesus, however, Noah unselfishly gave one hundred years of his life to build the ark. There is no way he would have spent that length of time on such a significant task just for his own sake. No, he was primarily dedicated to the well-being of others.

When we are primarily dedicated to the well-being of others, it is amazing the vision God will plant in our hearts.

Third, a friendship with God is a gift because a friendship is a relationship in which people are interdependent upon each other.

When my brother was in the Army and stationed in Germany many years ago, he bought us a cuckoo clock. It is not just a fabulous clock. It is a beautiful piece of artwork. The hand-carved pendulum of the clock goes back and forth and, if set correctly, keeps excellent time. The movement of the pendulum is symbolic of many aspects of life. One aspect is our relationship with God. Think of one side of the pendulum swing as total independence from God. Many people choose to live their lives this way, and everyone around them knows the chaos and tragedy that is left in the wake of such a life. Most people do not fully comprehend that they are not the only ones who pay the consequence of their sin.

"The Lord saw how great man's wickedness on the earth had become, and that every inclination of the thoughts of his heart was only evil all the time....So the Lord said, 'I will wipe mankind, whom I have created, from the face of the earth – men and animals and creatures that move along the ground, and birds of the air – for I am grieved that I have made them.'" (Genesis 6:5, 7). Who is the word "them" referring to at the end of verse 7? I believe it refers to humankind. Was God grieved because He made the animals? No. Did the animals, creatures, and birds sin against God? No. However, all of creation paid the consequences of human sin.

The same dynamic happens today. When we choose to live independently from God—with one decision or with many—we are not the only one who pays the consequences.

The consequences are not always immediate.

They are not always visible.

But they always happen.

The middle of the pendulum swing represents total dependence on God. At first glance it might sound like this should be the goal of our life. After all, don't we want to be totally dependent upon God? Yes we do. However, the middle of the pendulum swing represents a life that is totally dependent upon God for everything, but God cannot depend on them for anything. The consequences of this type of life can also be tragic. The disastrous consequences usually manifest themselves in future generations. The person who lives their life in the middle of the pendulum swing normally puts God at a high priority only in times of difficulty or crisis. During these times, God and spiritual disciplines become a priority. These stay a priority until the crisis is gone, then both outward and inward commitment fades quickly.

People who live their lives in the middle of the pendulum swing don't normally see the negative consequences of their behavior. This is because the negative consequences normally manifest in the next generation. Children who live in an environment where sporadic commitment is the norm begin to wonder about the value of faith for all of life. To them it is hypocritical behavior because deep commitment is not seen consistently. It is rarely something they want in their life. It is not uncommon for the next generation to turn away from the faith entirely if the previous generation lives in the middle of the pendulum swing.

This dynamic is seen in one of the saddest passages in the entire Bible:

> *The people served the Lord throughout the lifetime of Joshua and of the elders who outlived him and who had seen all the great things the Lord had done for Israel....After that whole generation had been gathered to their fathers, another generation grew up, who knew neither the Lord nor what he had done for Israel. Then the Israelites did evil in the eyes of the Lord and served the Baals. They forsook the Lord, the God of their fathers, who had brought them out of Egypt. They followed and worshipped various gods of the peoples around them. They provoked the Lord to anger... (Judges 2:7, 10–12).*

What we see in this tragic passage is that it only took two generations after Joshua for people to turn away from God. It was at this time that God raised up judges:

> *Whenever the Lord raised up a judge for them, He was with the judge and saved them out of the hands of their enemies as long as the judge lived; for the Lord had compassion on them as they groaned under those who oppressed and afflicted them. But when the judge died, the people returned to ways even more corrupt than those of their fathers, following other gods and serving and worshipping them. They refused to give up their evil practices and stubborn ways* (Judges 2:18–19).

What history shows is that when we live in total dependence upon God only in times of crisis, it is common for the next generation to do the same. However, each generation also chooses to live in greater and greater independence from God. Much of what is happening in our country today is a result of this dynamic.

There is another option for life. It is interdependence upon God. It is when we totally depend upon God all the time, and He totally depends upon us all the time. It is this type of life that is lived on the opposite side of the pendulum swing from total independence. There are internal and external forces that keep a pendulum from staying on one side of the swing. There are also internal and external forces that work to keep us from being interdependent upon God. Anyone who has ever tried to be interdependent upon God can give testimony to that fact. It was this type of life that Noah chose to live, and it would be a worthy goal for anyone.

When people talk about their relationship with God through His Son, Jesus, it is not uncommon to hear words like: my faith in Him; my hope in Him; my trust and confidence is in Him. When we see a bigger picture of an interdependent relationship, then it is important to know that God also has faith in us. He has hope in us. He also has trust and confidence in us.

Noah had five hundred years to perfect his interdependence on God! We have no way of knowing how the relationship between God and Noah grew so strong. Obviously it was a choice both of them made. (The truth is that God always makes that choice and waits for us to do the same.)

The day finally came when God knew that Noah's interdependence had grown so strong he could now be trusted with a vision beyond comprehension. However, a big vision is not the only aspect of this type of relationship. Since God was silent during the entire construction of the ark, Noah had to have total confidence in the One who spoke the vision: *"Noah did everything just as God commanded him"* (Genesis 6:22).

In the New Testament, there is a growing interdependence between Jesus and the disciples. Before He even called his first disciple, He knew about the task of finding people who would follow Him, helping them grow until they became interdependent with Him, and then leaving them with the vision of taking the Gospel to the ends of the earth.

Did they, or do we, ever become totally interdependent? No. If we choose, however, we can grow in our understanding, our willingness, our faith, and our commitment. We, like the disciples, have the option of relying upon the Holy Spirit. I say "option," but in reality the more interdependent we become the more we are open to supplement:

- our wisdom with the wisdom of the Holy Spirit
- our power with the power of the Holy Spirit
- our heart with the heart of the Holy Spirit
- our priorities with the priorities of the Holy Spirit
- our motives with the motives of the Holy Spirit

Friendship with God is not just for the few. He offers it to all. All who are willing to make the commitment to that friendship will joyfully discover that a friendship with God is a gift we can't afford to lose.

Questions

■ Many people are afraid of developing friendships. Why?

■ Who are your closest friends?

■ How did Noah have a friendship with God?

■ How can you?

■ What does it mean to be interdependent?

Gift Nine

Righteousness

This is the account of Noah.

Noah was a righteous man, blameless among the people of his time, and he walked with God...

The LORD then said to Noah, "Go into the ark, you and your whole family, because I have found you righteous in this generation."

—Genesis 6:9, 7:1

The inaugural Albuquerque International Balloon Fiesta took place when I was a senior in high school. I don't remember how many hot air balloons there were the first year. However, I do remember leaving class early with a few friends and going to watch the balloons. From the very first glance at one of those unique aircraft, I have enjoyed watching hot air balloons. Over the years, the shapes and sizes have changed, but the fascination of watching them has never diminished.

One by one the colorful balloons inflated and rose to a vertical position. Every balloon was unique and we watched with wide eyes and big smiles as the balloons ascended, then disappeared over the horizon.

Recently, my wife, Diana, and I went to the Plano Balloon Festival north of Dallas, Texas. There were over sixty balloons and it was a fantastic afternoon. We walked around the vendor area while the balloon crews were unloading their trailers. At a designated time, the balloon crews were given a signal and the first group of thirty began to fill their balloons with hot air. One by one the colorful balloons inflated and rose to a vertical position. Every balloon was unique and we watched with wide eyes and big smiles as the balloons ascended, then disappeared over the horizon.

About two hours later, the second group of thirty balloons was unloaded and waited for the signal to begin filling. I was even more fascinated with this second group because, by then, the sun had set. We heard from the announcer that the balloons were not going to fly at night. Rather, they were there for the spectators to view and for an "all burn." I had never heard of an all burn, so I was anxious to know what was going to happen.

After thirty minutes, all the balloons were filled and vertical. The announcer told the crowd that in one minute there would be an all burn. I was more than excited to see what that was going to mean. Then the announcer said, "All burn in ten, nine, eight, seven, six, five, four, three, two, one. All burn!" At that moment, one of the most fascinating sights I have ever seen was there before my eyes. An all burn is when all the balloon pilots simultaneously turn on the flame to fill their balloons with hot air. We never saw that during the daylight, but at night it was a totally different story. During the daylight, the balloons are beautiful, but at night they are radiant. At night the flame makes the balloon glow from the inside out. Since every balloon was different and the all burn lasted only about fifteen seconds, it was over before I could move my stare from the balloon closest to us. There were several more all burns, then a "twinkle burn," where the flames only lasted about two seconds on, then ten seconds off. Since not all the balloons were twinkling at the same time, the field before us looked like giant lightening bugs at a birthday party.

I sat there mesmerized.

Then the announcer said he was going to let us do something that had never been done before at that balloon festival. He said that since there was no wind, we could go down on the field next to the balloons. I was like a kid in a candy store and got right next to the balloons. I even looked up inside some of them. That was something that I had never done, even in those early days of the balloon festival in Albuquerque.

Several days later, my experience with the balloons helped me to better understand one of the most important lessons of the entire

Bible—the lesson of righteousness. This lesson is important because righteousness is a gift we can't afford to lose.

In Genesis 6:9, we read, *"Noah was a righteous man, blameless, among the people of his time, and he walked with God."* Then in Genesis 7:1, we read, *"The Lord then said to Noah, 'Go into the ark, you and your whole family, because I have found you righteous in this generation.'"* Even though there were one hundred years of time between those two verses, Noah is still righteous. In the Old Testament, the word righteous means living so that the consequences of our actions bring favorable results to others. As a righteous man, Noah chose to live in such a way that his thoughts, motives, actions, and the consequences of those actions were favorable to God and people.

However, there is a significant difference between righteous and righteousness. Being righteous is an adjective, which describes human behavior that has favorable consequences to others. On the other hand, righteousness is a noun that describes our position before God. Being righteous is something we can create on our own. Righteousness is something that only God alone can give us and is in response to our faith in Him.

In Genesis 15:6, we read one of the most important passages on this topic in the entire Bible: *"Abram believed the Lord, and he credited it to him as righteousness."* This passage emphasizes the fact that God responded to Abram's faith by crediting righteousness to him. Abram was not the one who took the initiative in the relationship between himself and God. No, it was God who took the initiative. When Abram responded in faith to God's initiative, then God responded by placing Abram in a right relationship with himself, which is called righteousness.

The same dynamic happened between God and Noah. Hebrews 11:7 says, *"By faith Noah, when warned about things not yet seen, in holy fear built an ark to save his family. By his faith he condemned the world and became heir of the righteousness that comes by faith."*

In Genesis 6:9, we read that *"Noah was a righteous man..."* It was his own behavior that gained him the reputation of a righteous man. However, it was through his faith in God that he became an heir of righteousness.

There are several important lessons to learn about righteousness.

First, righteousness is a free gift to us and therefore we cannot earn it.

Recently I coordinated a surprise birthday party for my wife, Diana. It took months to plan. I needed help from about a dozen good friends to make it a total surprise and for it to be the best experience possible. The invitations were mailed telling people when to arrive and where to park. From the time a friend picked her up for lunch, we had two and a half hours to decorate the house and get it ready for sixty-five guests. People were more than willing to help make it an experience of a lifetime. I paid for the food and decorations, but everyone helped out because they loved Diana and they wanted to help to make this "gift" to her very special.

We could have celebrated her birthday without the party, or decorations, or friends. However, I wanted to give her that visible gift as a way of showing my love to her.

Read these words about Jesus: *"He was chosen before the creation of the world, but was revealed in these last times for your sake"* (1 Peter 1:20). Can you imagine the discussion about salvation that went on

127

in heaven before the creation of the world? Isn't it awe-inspiring to think that prior to creation every detail of God's gift to us in Christ had been planned? Nothing was left undone, and best of all, no one's need for salvation has been overlooked. When Jesus came, His life, death, and resurrection were all a visible reality of God's gift of love to us.

Since Jesus' love is a gift, we cannot earn it. Since we are sinful, we do not deserve it. His unconditional love comes to us in the midst of our sinfulness and offers a personal relationship with Himself. When we respond in faith to Jesus' initiative of love, we become an heir of His righteousness. That is why Paul said, *"This righteousness from God comes through faith in Jesus Christ to all who believe"* (Romans 3:22). This gift of righteousness is officially called *imputed* righteousness because we cannot obtain righteousness simply by being righteous. Instead, when we recognize the reality of Isaiah 64:6 that *"our righteous acts are like filthy rags,"* then we will also recognize the reality of Philippians 3:9, *"...not having a righteousness of my own that comes from the law, but that which is through faith in Christ—the righteousness that comes from God and is by faith."*

A great example of this gift of righteousness is found in one of the most well-known parables of Jesus. It is commonly called the parable of the prodigal son and is found in Luke 15:11–32.

I believe this parable has been given the wrong title. Instead of focusing on the action of the son, the real focus should be on the loving action of the father. This is, after all, a parable about our loving heavenly Father and His willingness to receive and forgive us regardless of whether we have squandered his gifts, our lives, or both.

There is an interesting phrase in Luke 15:17 (NRSV) that is only used in that verse and in one other verse of the Bible; that being Acts 12:11. The phrase is, he *"came to himself."* In Acts 12, the phrase is used after an angel helped Peter escape from prison. In Luke 15, the phrase is used while the son was feeding pigs, while he, himself, was starving. In Luke 15:17, the New International Version super-ficially translates this phrase as *"he came to his senses,"* which could mean that he basically just had a cognitive experience in the midst of the pigs. However, his actions in the rest of the story suggest that he had more than just a cognitive experience. I believe he experienced the godly sorrow that Paul mentioned in 2 Corinthians 7:10, *"Godly sorrow brings repentance that leads to salvation."* It is godly sorrow that produces humility. It is godly sorrow that produces a willingness to admit mistakes and ask for forgiveness. It is godly sorrow that also produces a desire to live differently afterward. Merely coming to our senses produces none of these.

In Luke 15:17, we read the son *"came to himself,"* and left the pigs and went to his father. If he had not also believed that his father was loving, merciful, forgiving, and compassionate, he never would have responded the way he did.

While the son was *"still a long way off,"* (Luke 15:20) his father saw him, ran to him, embraced him, and kissed him. Then the father said to his servants, *"Bring the best robe and put it on him. Put a ring on his finger, and sandals on his feet"* (Luke 15:22). The best robe in the house was the one worn by the father. The father gave his son a gift he had not earned and did not deserve. The son received that gift because he chose to respond to the love of the father which had always been present.

You and I can come to ourselves and respond to the love of the heavenly Father by receiving Jesus Christ as our Savior. When we do, the heavenly Father will robe us with His robe of righteousness that we cannot earn simply by being righteous.

In Luke 15, the son also received a ring and sandals. The ring was a sign of authority, and only children of the father wore sandals; the servants did not. When we respond to God's love for us by accepting Jesus, we become a child of God, an heir—*"heirs of God and co-heirs with Christ"* (Romans 8:17).

Second, righteousness is a free gift to us, but it was not a free gift for us—it cost Jesus his life.

The tragedy of 9/11 will forever live in our nation's memory. On that horrible day, there were hundreds of stories of heroism in the Twin Towers, on the ground, in the Pentagon, and in the air. Perhaps one of the best-known stories is that of Todd Beamer. Faced with an incredible challenge, he and others gave their lives so that many more lives would be saved. His famous words, "Let's roll," still remain as words of bravery and courage. Todd Beamer did not have much time to decide what he was going to do. When a decision was made and action taken, the sacrifice to give his life for others was consistent with how he chose to live.

Jesus was born, grew up, and freely gave his life to die on a cross so we could have forgiveness of our sins. The sacrifice at the end was consistent with how He chose to live—for others.

When we accept Jesus as our personal Savior and Lord, we are clothed with His righteousness. It is important, but difficult, to comprehend that this imputed righteousness that is given to us as a gift—because we cannot earn it—cost Jesus everything; yet He willingly gave His life for us.

Third, righteousness is a gift that transforms us.

One of the most beautiful and fascinating places my wife and I have seen is Butchart Gardens in Brentwood Bay, Vancouver Island, British Columbia, Canada. We had heard of the gardens from friends who had visited there. However, until we visited ourselves and saw the beauty with our own eyes, it was hard to imagine. The history of the gardens is almost as fascinating as the gardens themselves.

In 1888, Robert Butchart, a native of Ontario, began manufacturing cement. In 1904, he moved to Tod Inlet on Vancouver Island. After several years, the limestone was completely removed from the quarry near their home. Robert's wife, Jennie, then had the idea of turning the rock pit into a beautiful garden. She acquired tons of topsoil from nearby farms and had it hauled to the pit by horse and cart. The soil was used to line the floor of the quarry. After the soil, plants and trees were added. Before long, the dull colorless pit was transformed into a beautiful sunken garden. Within a few years a Japanese garden was added near their home, and then an Italian garden and rose garden were also added.

In the 1920s, over 50,000 people visited the beautiful gardens each year. Butchart Garden's popularity has continued to grow. Today, more than one million people visit each year (www.butchartgardens.com).

Isn't it amazing what can happen when one person has a vision of turning an empty rock pit into something beautiful? But Jennie Butchart did not just have a vision. She also took action to make her vision a reality. Without the action, the vision would have been short-lived. Without the vision, there would have been no need for action. Her vision and action worked in tandem to bring about transformation.

That is the same dynamic that happened with God, our heavenly Father. God did not work with a rock pit, but He did work with a pile of dust in which He created human life. Everything was fine until Adam and Eve chose to sin. Since that time, it has been God's desire for humankind to be back in a relationship with Himself. God chooses to love us right where we are and just the way we are. However, after we respond to His love, it is important for us to realize that God loves us too much to let us remain as we are. His vision of our transformation to be more like Jesus is accompanied by the action of the Holy Spirit that works within us to bring about this transformation. *"And we, who with unveiled faces all reflect the Lord's glory, are being transformed into His likeness with ever-increasing glory, which comes from the Lord, who is the Spirit"* (2 Corinthians 3:18).

It is God's desire to transform our pile of dust into a beautiful garden that continually reflects His beauty.

It is God's desire to transform our pile of dust into a beautiful garden that continually reflects His beauty.

My second-favorite Psalm is Psalm 1. In verses 1–3 we read, *"Blessed is the man who does not walk in the counsel of the wicked or stand in the way of sinners or sit in the seat of mockers. But his delight is in the law of the Lord, and on his law he mediates day and night. He is like a tree planted by streams of water, which yields its fruit in season and whose leaf does not wither. Whatever he does prospers."*

The righteousness of God is a gift we cannot afford to lose because His righteousness and the work of the Holy Spirit transform us from a pile of dust into beautiful children of God.

Questions

- What did you think about when reading the story of the balloons?

- How did Noah become righteous?

- What are your thoughts about the line: "righteous-ness is a free gift to us and therefore we cannot earn it"?

- What keeps us from believing that truth?

- What would Jesus say about it?

10

Gift Ten

Family

When Methuselah had lived 187 years, he became the father of Lamech. And after he became the father of Lamech, Methuselah lived 782 years and had other sons and daughters. Altogether, Methuselah lived 969 years, and then he died.

When Lamech had lived 182 years, he had a son. He named him Noah and said, "He will comfort us in the labor and painful toil of our hands caused by the ground the LORD has cursed." After Noah was born, Lamech lived 595 years and had other sons and daughters. Altogether, Lamech lived 777 years, and then he died.

After Noah was 500 years old, he became the father of Shem, Ham and Japheth.

—Genesis 5:25–32

Many years ago, Diana and I told our children that we would take them to all the states before they graduated from high school. Little did we realize the promise we had made. When we told them all the states, they took us literally. We meant all of the lower forty-eight states. However, when you say "all" to a child, you better mean all.

Once we made that promise, it was a goal that brought excitement to our family. Every summer, and many spring break vacations, we went on trips to accomplish that goal. All those trips took planning. Some took a few weeks to plan; others took months. The older our children got, the more input they had into which states we visited when, and what we did when we got there. We have dozens of photo albums and countless memories of our travels.

Early in our travels, I went to a motor home dealership and bought a map that goes on the outside of a motor home. It was a map with different colored stickers for each state. I mounted the map on a piece of Plexiglas, and we hung it in a very visible place in our home.

After returning from a trip, we would take the map off the wall and let the kids place the appropriate stickers on the map for the states we had visited. That map quickly became a visual reminder of the promise and its fulfillment.

We soon began to hang pictures around the map. These pictures are some of our best memories of places we have been—whether that be a picture of us rafting down a river in Colorado, standing on a dock in San Francisco, dog sledding in Alaska, or standing on a beach in Hawaii.

Planning for and going on vacations did not consume our life, but it did give our family a goal that required focus, commitment, and over ten years to accomplish. For several years, Diana and I wondered how we were going to tell the kids we could not afford to go to Alaska or Hawaii because it was just too expensive. However, even that goal was reached because of miraculous events and the generosity of friends who gave us airline tickets or air miles.

That map continues to hang on the wall in our home. Beside it is a picture of Diana, Matt, and Trisha holding the map and sitting in front of a giant chocolate chip cookie. It is a picture that I took the night we put the last sticker on the map and celebrated the accomplishment of fulfilling our promise. It is because of these and many other experiences that I have come to the conclusion that family is a gift we can't afford to lose.

First, family is a gift because our family should be our primary environment for faith development.

I have a great memory from the night my family celebrated the completion of our United States travels and placed the last sticker on our map. On several occasions since that night of celebration, I have wondered how our family—especially our children—has been influenced by our travels. We can only speculate on how our family would be different if we had never traveled. After all, there are so many factors that have an influence on families. Some are positive factors and some are negative factors. Some of the factors happen in the immediate family and some in the extended family.

It would be impossible to list all the factors that both positively and negatively influence our family, but some of them are:

- affirmation
- encouragement
- goals
- death
- faith
- relocation
- health
- fun
- finances
- peer pressure
- expectations
- attitude

In the midst of an increased level of busyness within families, it seems that some parents attempt to get their children involved in every activity possible. For other parents, the busyness revolves around their employment, and their children are neglected.

A logical question that arises is this: what kind of influence is all this busyness having on families? We would be naïve to say it has none. That would be like saying all of our family travels had no influence on our family. When Diana and I first began to plan these trips, we wanted to finish traveling to all the states before our children graduated from high school. The primary reason for that timeline was that we wanted to give each of our kids a very unique high school graduation present. They could pick their favorite place we had visited, and we would go back there again. Diana and I thought it was a great idea, and we told the kids and reminded them of it at least once a year.

We finished traveling to the last state in the summer of 2001. It was the summer before our son's senior year of high school. Diana and I thought that the timing was perfect. Now all Matt had to do was decide where he wanted to go the following summer, and we would begin making plans to return to that place.

Several months went by and Matt said nothing except that he was thinking about it. Then one day he made his announcement, "I want to go to Australia!" Then he said, "And I want to go with some of my friends." Over the next few weeks, as we negotiated about that desire, several questions came to my mind. "Who influenced him to think outside the box? Who birthed in him a spirit of adventure? When did he develop the initiative to get a job and the discipline to save money to pay for half the trip? What caused him to ask for a camera for his birthday so he could make a photo album of his adventure, just like Mom does?"

How do the things we do or not do influence the faith development of our family?

His trip to Australia was incredible for him. Through that experience, Diana and I learned so much about our influence on our children. Two years later, when our daughter Trisha graduated and decided she wanted to go to London and Paris, we were not surprised.

If traveling around the country can have that much influence on children—influence in ways we didn't realize until later—then my question is this: how do the things we do or not do influence the faith development of our family? Our activities and priorities do influence the faith development of our family. I have heard it said more than once that a major reason teenagers begin smoking is because they see their parents smoke. If that is true, then is it too difficult to conclude that a major reason a child or teenager would take faith seriously is because they see it modeled in their parents?

What was it in Noah's family that helped lay a foundation for him to become a man of such faith? In addition, what foundation did he lay that enabled his descendants to be people of faith?

In order to answer these questions, we need to look at Noah's genealogy. Beginning in Genesis 5:21, we read about the three generations prior to Noah. These three generations included: Enoch, Methuselah, and Lamech. This part of Noah's genealogy is illustrated in **Chart 3: Genealogy**.

Chart 3
Genealogy Chart
(Genesis 5:21-32)

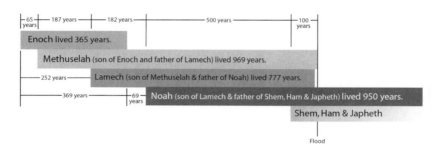

What is not illustrated in Chart 3 is what we read about Enoch in Genesis 5:22 and 5:24. In verse 22, we read these words, *"And after he became the father of Methuselah, Enoch **walked with God** 300 years and had other sons and daughters"* (emphasis added). *In verse 24, we read, "Enoch **walked with God;** then he was no more, because God took him away"* (emphasis added).

The words, *"walked with God,"* that describe Enoch's life, are the exact same Hebrew words that are used to describe Noah's life in Genesis 6:9 where we read, *"Noah was a righteous man, blameless among people of his time, and he walked with God."*

From Chart 3 we see that Noah was born sixty-nine years after God took Enoch away. I do not know if Enoch's walk with God had much influence on his son, Methuselah, or on his grandson, Lamech. However, I believe that Enoch's life had a significant influence on Noah. The Hebrew people are passionate in orally passing down the traditions of the faith to their families. I can only imagine that as young Noah began to grow up and be inquisitive, he asked all kinds of questions and was told incredible stories about his great-grandfather, who *"was no more, because God took him"* (Genesis 5:24).

I believe it was Enoch who helped lay the foundation and provide an environment of faith development for young Noah. I came to that conclusion based on the information illustrated in Chart 3. From the words in Genesis 5, which are illustrated in the genealogy chart, we see that Methuselah died the year of the flood. It is my opinion that he did not just die the same year as the flood, but rather died in the flood along with all the other skeptics of his day. If he was not a skeptic, then he must have believed in the vision that God gave Noah. If he believed in the vision, why was he not on the ark? If he believed in the vision, why did he choose to die by drowning? It is my opinion that Methuselah was a skeptic and could talk about the faith of his father, Enoch, but he did not allow it to influence him enough to incorporate it personally into his life. So the faith was in his family environment, but not in him personally. I believe the same dynamic could have been true for Noah's father, Lamech. Like Methuselah, Lamech was in an environment of faith and could talk about it, but might not have incorporated it into his life. It is hard to know, considering he died five years before the flood. If Lamech was a man of faith, then Noah got to see faith modeled in his house instead of just having faith talked about. That was also true for some of Noah's descendants and continues to be true in many families today. One generation lives with incredible faith and creates an incredible environment of faith for the family. However, for some reason the future generations choose not to incorporate the family's faith into their personal life. As a result, there is tragedy just like in the life of Methuselah.

In **Chart 4: From Noah to Abraham** (on the next page), we see the ten generations after Noah, which are written in Genesis 10 and 11. Before the genealogy begins in Genesis 10, we read these words in Genesis 9:28–29, *"After the flood Noah lived 350 years. Altogether, Noah lived 950 years, and then he died."*

In Chart 4 we see that Abraham was the tenth generation after Noah. What is amazing is that Abraham was born only 292 years after the flood while Noah was still alive! In fact, Abraham was fifty-eight years old when Noah died. In addition, between the fifth generation (Peleg) and the sixth generation, (Reu) after Noah, the Tower of Babel happened, which is recorded in Genesis 11.

It is my opinion that God kept Noah alive for a long time for a very specific reason. Noah was the man who continually provided the faith environment for the family through the tragedy of the Tower of Babel and into a significant portion of Abraham's life.

Chart 4
From Noah to Abraham
(Genesis 9:28-29, 11:10-32, 21:1-5, 25:7-8)

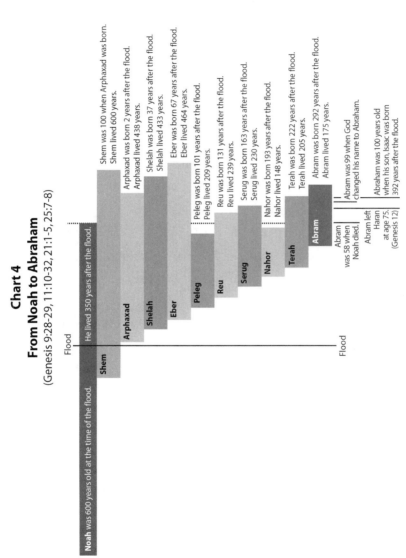

Flood

Noah was 600 years old at the time of the flood.

He lived 350 years after the flood.

Shem

Shem was 100 when Arphaxad was born.
Shem lived 600 years.

Arphaxad

Arphaxad was born 2 years after the flood.
Arphaxad lived 438 years.

Shelah

Shelah was born 37 years after the flood.
Shelah lived 433 years.

Eber

Eber was born 67 years after the flood.
Eber lived 464 years.

Peleg

Peleg was born 101 years after the flood.
Peleg lived 209 years.

Reu

Reu was born 131 years after the flood.
Reu lived 239 years.

Serug

Serug was born 163 years after the flood.
Serug lived 230 years.

Nahor

Nahor was born 193 years after the flood.
Nahor lived 148 years.

Terah

Terah was born 222 years after the flood.
Terah lived 205 years.

Abram

Abram was born 292 years after the flood.
Abram lived 175 years.

Abram was 58 when Noah died.

Abram left Haran at age 75. (Genesis 12)

Abram was 99 when God changed his name to Abraham.

Abraham was 100 years old when his son, Isaac was born 392 years after the flood.

Flood

I am not suggesting that Abraham ever met Noah. If they did not meet, it can be safely assumed that Abraham heard story after story of this great man of faith named Noah, who was a living example of faith for the first fifty-eight years of Abraham's life.

After all, who provided the faith that influenced Abraham to recognize the voice of God when He spoke? The Scripture does not record anyone of any generation between Noah and Abraham that had the kind of faith both Noah and Abraham displayed in their lives.

If is my belief that it is not recorded because that kind of faith was not present in any generation between Noah and Abraham. In this day and time, as in the Biblical generations, significant lives of faith might skip a generation or two. But since family is a gift we can't afford to lose, it is crucial for every generation of every family to share faith stories and do all they can to provide an environment for faith development.

Second, family is a gift because it is within the family that we learn values that help us succeed in the world.

Every family does not always contain or model every value which needs to be learned. In addition, every family does not always know how to share faith stories that will inspire faith development. These are two of the many reasons why involvement in a church family is so important. Involvement in a healthy church allows values to be seen and copied by people of all ages. It is not accurate to assume that someone's biological age is a good indicator of their maturity of faith. So by involvement in a church family, children and adults can learn from each other about values that help us succeed in the world.

What are these values to which I am referring? A good list would include: servant values, social values, moral values, work values, and ethical values. In addition, there are the values of integrity, honesty, responsibility, and financial accountability.

Whose responsibility is it to teach and pass on values from one generation to the next? I believe it is the relational family and the church family. Very few, if any, of these values can be taught and passed on as the result of a cognitive exercise alone. They need to be taught and caught— taught by verbal instruction and caught by modeling these values every day.

Earlier in this chapter I referred to a miraculous event that enabled my family to go to Hawaii. Through that event, our entire family learned more about the value of giving and sharing and about the spiritual value of reaping and sowing.

In 1983, I bought a 1955 Ford F-100 pickup truck. It has been a project truck ever since. Some of my family believed the truck really did not exist, and others believed it would never be finished. From the beginning, Diana and I made an agreement as to how I would pay for this restoration project. I would use money from weddings, funerals, outside speaking engagements, or love offerings to pay for improvements to the truck.

Working on this project was fun. But it was slow because the extra money was not predictable. In December 1998, I was invited to a home Bible study group of people from the church. That particular night, a missionary to Africa was there to speak about his work. As he spoke, he told about how much of the work he did required the use of a small airplane to travel to remote villages. The reason he had come back to the United States was to raise money for another airplane. About two months before, his son had flown the plane to a remote village and died when the plane crashed on the return flight.

I was in the back of the crowd that night, literally standing in the entryway of the home. When the missionary finished speaking he told how we could give money to help him get a new plane. I asked the Lord, "What do you want me to do about this?" I felt the Lord say, "I want you to give him the truck money that is in the envelope on your dresser."

Since I did not get a lot of money for my truck at any one time, I kept it in an envelope on my dresser. On that particular night, I did not know exactly how much money was in the envelope because it had been many months since I had put any money in it.

I told the Lord, "No, I'm not giving my truck money. You know how long it takes me to get money for that."

The Lord said, "Give him your truck money."

I said, "No, Lord, not the truck money."

By this time the missionary had finished speaking. Everyone else was beginning to walk around and talk to one another. I was still in the entryway discussing this with the Lord.

After several more minutes of conversation and self-examination, I finally said, "Okay, Lord, I'll give the truck money, but I do not even know how much money is in the envelope."

I felt the Lord say, "That's the whole point."

I went home that night, told Diana what had happened and counted the truck money. To my shock there was $1,150 in the envelope.

The next day I took the money over to the person who was collecting it for the missionary. That night, I met Diana at church for our normal Wednesday night dinner. Behind us in line was a couple. About two weeks before, the man had retired from the airline business.

As we were talking he said, "We have been thinking about something and are glad we can talk to both of you tonight. I just retired and have all these airline tickets that will allow me to fly anywhere in the world. We would like to give you two of them." He then handed me an envelope. Diana and I stood there in shock. "Thank you," was all we could say.

On the inside I was saying to myself, "Lord, why was it so hard to trust You with the truck money, when all You want to do is bless me?"

The next day we told our children the story of the truck money and the airline tickets. Needless to say, they were excited because they could see those tickets with Hawaii written all over them.

About a week later, the same retired airline executive called me and said, "Dean, I've been thinking. With only two tickets, that means you will have to buy two more. So we're going to give you two more tickets."

I was just as shocked then as I was the week before. When I got off the phone, I made a quick calculation in my head. I gave $1,150 to the Lord for a missionary I might not ever meet again. Within one week, the Lord blessed my family with airline tickets worth four times that much.

That night when we told our kids about the other tickets, they were ready to pack their bags and leave immediately.

Diana and I will never know how much that experience will influence our children. We know it did influence them because one day when Matt was in college, he told us he had decided to give 20 percent of his monthly income to his church. Then Trisha told us that in addition to tithing, she was supporting a child through World Vision.

How could we respond to our children? Should we have said, "What are you doing? Why are you giving so much money away?"

Or should we have realized that the values they learned were of far greater significance than how to plan a trip.

Families are a gift we can't afford to lose because with the family we learn values that help us succeed in the world.

Third, families are a gift because within the family we can learn good values.

What are these values to which I am referring? They are values like:

- Love has no boundaries.
- Questions can always be asked.
- Differences can be addressed.
- Hurts can be reconciled.
- Disappointments can be shared.
- Victories can be cherished.
- Plans can be made.
- Dreams can be lived.
- Forgiveness is crucial.
- Humor is vital.

From my experience, both good and bad values are like a crease in a piece of paper. Both types of values are hard to get rid of once they are there. That is why it is so important to teach good values at an early age. That is another reason a good church family is so crucial because they can reinforce good values.

Unfortunately, our experience as a pastoral family has not always been positive. After one difficult time at church, Diana was asked by one of our children, "If Christians are supposed to be so loving, why are those people saying such mean things about Daddy?"

Even though we tried to keep the church struggles away from our children, it was impossible to do so all the time. Children are like radars and sponges all at the same time. Like radars, they pick up on changes in our tone of voice, our energy level, and our mood, without us ever realizing it. Like sponges, they absorb more than we realize, even if they are in their rooms and their doors are closed.

In the story of Noah we can only guess about some of the values that Noah and his wife tried to teach their children. Some of these values could have been: prayer is crucial, vision is vital, hope is essential, planning is important, and hard work is necessary. At the end of the story of Noah we see that two of Noah's sons had also developed the value of respect. After the flood, Noah planted a vineyard (Genesis 9:20–27). From the grapes he made wine, got drunk, and lay uncovered inside his tent. His son, Ham, saw him and told his two brothers. In verse 23 we read, *"But Shem and Japheth took a garment and laid it across their shoulders; they then walked in backward and covered their father's nakedness."*

When Noah awoke, he cursed Ham's son, Canaan, and blessed Shem and Japheth. Where and how did these two sons learn respect for their father, while the other son made fun of him? We will never know. The dynamics of learning values were the same in Noah's family as they are in ours. Children learn by watching us live and copying our behavior. Maybe Ham was influenced by someone who died in the flood more than he was influenced by Noah. We don't know. What we do know is that the curse placed on Canaan because of Ham's lack of respect lasted for generations. The same was true for the blessing given to Shem and Japheth.

How do children learn good values if we do not teach them? How do they learn to love and respect people, especially the elderly, if we do not show them? How do our children learn to hold the door open for others if they never see it happen? How do our children learn the importance of play or humor if everything is so strict and serious? How do they learn about forgiveness if we never ask them to forgive us for mistakes we have made in their lives? When will they learn to share their deepest feelings, disappointments, hurts, or dreams unless they see us do the same? When do they learn about boundaries if we do not practice them or enforce the ones we give them?

The list can go on and on. That is why I believe that families are a gift we can't afford to lose because it is within our families that we learn good values.

Questions

- Describe some of your favorite memories from your times of traveling.

- What pictures come to your mind?

- How can family be our primary environment for faith development?

■ What keeps that from happening?

■ How do the things we do or not do influence the faith development of our family?

11

Gift Eleven

Godself

And God said, "This is the sign of the covenant I am making between me and you and every living creature with you, a covenant for all generations to come: I have set my rainbow in the clouds, and it will be the sign of the covenant between me and the earth. Whenever I bring clouds over the earth and the rainbow appears in the clouds, I will remember my covenant between me and you and all living creatures of every kind. Never again will the waters become a flood to destroy all life. Whenever the rainbow appears in the clouds, I will see it and remember the everlasting covenant between God and all living creatures of every kind on the earth."

So God said to Noah, "This is the sign of the covenant I have established between me and all life on the earth."

—Genesis 9:12–17

Many years ago when I was a junior at Baylor University, I had a very powerful and scary experience. That year, I lived at the Methodist Children's Home in Waco, Texas, and was the assistant home parent to eighteen senior high school boys. One Saturday morning, I drove out to the Boy's Ranch to help set some concrete forms for new sidewalks. It had been raining all night, and it was still raining when I got up. I did not feel like getting out in the rain and going to the ranch, but I had promised that I would be there to help. So, I got out of bed, dressed, and went out in the pouring rain. I got into my 1965 Ford Falcon and drove to the ranch.

About a mile before the ranch, the road crossed a creek. The only way across the creek was a narrow, one-lane bridge. I got to the bridge and started to drive across, just like I had done many times before. For some reason something felt different when I got to the middle of the bridge. All of a sudden I heard a loud noise and the front of my car just dropped. The next day, I found out that the wood of the bridge had broken and my two front tires had landed on two wood beams that crossed the creek to hold up the bridge.

However, at that moment, I opened my car door to see what happened and saw that the water from the creek had risen to the bottom of my car. I got out and walked back across the bridge, as the water continued to rise.

That day I never made it to my destination. I also do not remember how I made it back to campus. The next day I met a tow truck driver at the bridge and had to pay him cash before he would pull my car off the bridge. For years after that incident I had a phobia about crossing any bridge.

There might not be too many people who have had the same experience I had on the bridge that day. However, the Bible teaches that all of us have experienced the same dynamics I did on that day. The Bible teaches that all of us are on a journey to find purpose and meaning in life. Whether we realize it or not, we will never find that purpose and meaning unless our journey is with God and God is our destination.

One of the realities that keep us away from our destination is the rising river of human sin. Sin is all encompassing, always destructive, always dangerous, and always stops us in our tracks.

That is one of the many reasons the story of Noah and the ark is so important. Even though the story obviously happened centuries before Jesus was born, God reveals Himself and His character in this story in a similar way He did in and through the life of Jesus. It is for this reason that God Himself, or Godself, is a gift we can't afford to lose. It is God who creates us. It is God who redeems us. It is God who empowers us to live daily.

First, Godself is a gift because it is God who creates us.

After Noah and his family left the ark, and before God told Noah about the rainbow, God spoke to Noah: *"For in the image of God, has God made man"* (Genesis 9:6). These words are very similar to those spoken by God in Genesis 1:26. The difference is that in Genesis 1, God spoke these words before any human being had been created. In Genesis 9, these words were spoken hundreds of years after creation and after the flood when Noah and his family were the only eight people on the earth. Why did God speak those words to Noah at that moment? What was the purpose of saying those words?

I believe that God wanted Noah to know that He (Godself) would still be involved in the creation of human life. He was not going to stop creating humankind, nor was He going to abandon humankind *"even though every inclination of his heart is evil from childhood"* (Genesis 8:21).

One evening many years ago, I went into Trisha's bedroom. I went through the tradition of tucking her in, kissing her goodnight, and saying I love you. Then what happened next is something I hope I always remember. She put her arms around my neck, pulled me as tight to her body as she could and said six words that, for me, have become six very special words. She said, "I will never let you go." Now, at that moment I was hoping that she would because I was being choked. I knew physically that was not true. She would eventually have to let me go, but I knew those words were from her heart. Since that time she has grown up and still continues to say those six words. I look forward to hearing those six words. It is my belief that it is not only my child that shares those six words with me. God also shares those six words with me. God also shares those six words with you. God says, "I will never let you go!" No matter what happens in your life, no matter what you do or don't do, God will never let you go.

That is the same reason God spoke those words to Noah (Genesis 9:6). He wanted Noah to know that in spite of human sin, failure, and weakness, God was not going to let humankind go.

Hundreds of years later, during the time of Jeremiah, the nation of Israel was once again paying the consequences of its own sinfulness. The time was about 586 BC, right before the Babylonian Empire destroyed the city of Jerusalem.

The prophet Jeremiah had been arrested and was held in captivity in the courtyard of the king. God spoke to Jeremiah and asked him to do something very unusual. God asked him to go out and buy a piece of property. Jeremiah did it. Even though Jeremiah would never see that property, the purchase was an action and a statement of Jeremiah's radical faith in a God who he knew would never let go of His people. In Jeremiah 32, we read the words of God that communicated the same message that was communicated to Noah in Genesis 9:6. We read in Jeremiah 32:36–38:

> *"You are saying about this city, 'By the sword, famine, and plague it will be handed over to the king of Babylon'; but this is what the Lord, the God of Israel says: I will surely gather them from all the lands where I banish them in my furious anger and great wrath; I will bring them back to this place and let them live in safety. They will be my people, and I will be their God."*

Why is God so consistently gracious and kind in the midst of human sinfulness? It is not only His character, but it is He, Godself, who creates us, so He will never let us go.

This same concept is again expressed in Titus 1:1–2: *"Paul, a servant of God and an apostle of Jesus Christ for the faith of God's elect and the knowledge of the truth that leads to godliness—a faith and knowledge resting on the hope of eternal life, which God, who does not lie, promised before the beginning of time."*

What Paul meant by these words is that long before God ever made a covenant with Noah, long before the earth was created, God had already made a covenant with you and me that is eternal. Before the creation of the world, God already knew He was going to make a covenant with His creation for the purpose of drawing us unto Himself. Why? Because He is not only willing to create us, He is not willing to let us go.

It is for this same reason that God was willing to send His Son to redeem us.

Second, Godself is a gift because it is God who redeems us.

There are some interesting parallels between the story of Noah and the story of Jesus. Those parallels are as follows:

Noah	Jesus
God spoke to Noah	God spoke through an angel to Mary and Joseph
God spoke about the ark	God spoke about Jesus
Noah was obedient	Mary and Joseph were obedient
Ark was built	Jesus was born
100 Years of time passed	33 Years of time passed
Procession of animals up into the ark	Procession of people up into Jerusalem on Palm Sunday
Flood covered the earth	Flood of human sin covered the earth
Rainbow as visible sign of covenant between God and humankind	Cross as visible sign of covenant between God and humankind.

From this comparison we see the Bible clearly teaches that God is the One who takes the initiative—always. We never take the initiative when it comes to God. We are always responding to the initiative He has already taken.

In the story of Noah, it was God who took the initiative to redeem His people. We do not know all the details as to how Noah managed to build the ark. But we do know why God gave him the vision, skill, resources, and determination. God did it to save His people.

Likewise, when the time was right, God took the initiative to be born as a human being whose name was Jesus. We do not know how the full divinity of God squeezed into the body of a human being. But we do know why. He did it to save us from our sins.

Let me once again refer to my experience of driving my car over the bridge when the bridge broke. In our life, in the midst of the rising river of our human sin, how do we build a bridge that will lead us to safety? How do we find a bridge that will lead us to safety? Very simply and honestly, we don't. We can never build a bridge by our own efforts, and we can never find the bridge by our own initiative.

The bridge was built for us.

The bridge always finds us.

In the midst of the rising river of human sin, we needed an indestructible bridge not made by human hands. We needed a bridge that could only be made and paid for by the blood-stained hands of the Son of God. Not only did God take the initiative for Jesus to be born at the right time but *"Christ died for sins once for all, the righteous for the unrighteous, to bring you to God"* (1 Peter 3:18).

In Jesus, God not only provided the bridge, but Godself was the bridge to redeem His people. So how do we cross the bridge that God has provided for us? Passage across the bridge involves a three-step process.

Step One: Confess Our Sin

There is a big difference between a mistake and a sin. One night, Diana and I were driving back home and we stopped at an ice cream parlor. We decided to split an ice cream cone. She picked the flavor of ice cream, and I picked the type of cone. I got it. I handed the cone to her, and I paid. She took a few licks of ice cream, handed it to me and said, "Since you are driving, why don't you hold it until we get to the car."

There were two exits out of that ice cream parlor. One exit went straight to the parking lot where we parked our car. The other exit forced you to go by a movie theater and all the way around the building. I started backing up as if I was going the long way by the movie theater. That way I could hold onto the ice cream cone that much longer. As soon as Diana realized what I was doing, I started laughing. I can guarantee she will never make that mistake again!

So many issues in life are like that. We make mistakes and hopefully learn from them so we never do them again. Jesus did not come to correct our mistakes. He came to save us from our sin. The rising river of human sin is rising because every one of us is adding to it. Until we are willing to acknowledge our own sinfulness and confess it to Jesus, we will never even acknowledge our own need for a bridge.

Step Two: Repentance and Asking Forgiveness

Repentance literally means to turn from sin. It means to make a U-turn away from sin and toward Jesus. While we are turning away from sin, it is crucial to ask for forgiveness. It is crucial to say, "Jesus, forgive me of my sin." We do not just say, "I'm sorry," because Jesus did not come and die just to accept our apology. He came to die to forgive us of our sin. When we ask forgiveness for whatever sin is in our life, forgiveness is instantly granted. At that same moment, we are picked up out of the river of sin by the powerful nail-pierced hands of Jesus, washed clean because of His blood, and helped to stand on the bridge of love that human sin can never destroy.

Step Three: Put Our Faith in Jesus

It takes faith to stand on the bridge named Jesus. Having faith in Jesus is not blind faith. It is faith in a Person:

- who was born for you and me
- who lived for you and me
- who died for you and me
- who was resurrected for you and me
- who sent His Spirit for you and me

Before we place our faith in Jesus, He already had faith in us.

- He believes you and I were worth His being born.
- He believes you and I were worth His living.
- He believes you and I were worth His dying.
- He believes you and I were worth His resurrection.
- He believes you and I were worth sending His Spirit.

The more we choose to put our faith in the One who first had faith in us, the more His Holy Spirit will burn away the desire we have for sin and put in us an increased desire to honor Jesus. It is Godself who forgives us.

Third, Godself is a gift because it is God who empowers us to live daily through the person of the Holy Spirit.

In Genesis 1:1–2 we read, *"In the beginning God created the heavens and the earth. Now the earth was formless and empty, darkness was over the surface of the deep, and the Spirit of God was hovering over the waters."*

Then in Genesis 6, just before the story of Noah, we read these words in verse 3, *"Then the Lord said, 'My Spirit will not contend with man forever, for he is mortal; his days will be a hundred and twenty years.'"*

The next time the spirit of God is mentioned is in Genesis 41:38, *"So Pharaoh asked them, 'can we find anyone like this man, one in whom is the spirit of God?'"*

My question is this: Where was the Spirit of God during Noah's life and during the time of the flood? Was He absent? Was He absent from Genesis 6 until Genesis 41:38? If we say yes, then we are saying that the Spirit of God was absent from the lives of Noah, Abraham, Isaac, and Jacob. That same line of argument would force us to conclude that the Spirit of God was not present and active in a person's life unless the words of the Old Testament specifically say so. I disagree with that conclusion. In the Old Testament, the Spirit of God was given to a particular person at a specific time for a specific task. So even though the Spirit of God is not mentioned at all in the story of Noah, He was not absent from Noah's life.

In the Old Testament when God gave someone a vision or a specific task, it was the Spirit of God who guided them, and empowered them with wisdom and energy to complete the task God had given. Thus, in Noah's life, it was the Spirit of God who first gave him the desire to live a righteous life before God. It was also the Spirit of God who guided Noah to pursue the vision of God, and also the Spirit of God who empowered him with wisdom and determination to complete the ark and live the vision God had given him.

What about you and me? In order to answer that question it is important to know that the Spirit of God interacts with people differently now than He did during the Old Testament times. Fifty days after Jesus' resurrection, the day of Pentecost was celebrated. This event is recorded in Acts 2. On that day, after the disciples experienced the presence and power of the Spirit of God—called the Holy Spirit— Peter boldly stood and referred to a prophecy from the Old Testament book of Joel when he said in Acts 2:17, *"In the last days, God says, I will pour out my Spirit **on all people"*** (emphasis added).

God was saying that no longer was the Spirit only available to certain people at certain times for certain tasks. From that moment on, the Holy Spirit would be available to all people at all times.

Since the Father, Son, and Holy Spirit are One (called the Trinity), it is my opinion that when we ask Jesus into our hearts to be our Lord and Savior, then He lives there through the power and presence of the Holy Spirit. However, just because the Holy Spirit is present in our lives does not mean we access His power for daily living.

When Diana and I lived in Atlanta during graduate school, we lived in a small, five-room house. In the middle of the house was a gas-fed floor furnace. During the cold months, the pilot light was kept lit, but the furnace would not roar into flame and heat the house until we adjusted the thermostat. The problem was that the thermostat was on the opposite side of the house. So in order to heat the house, someone (usually me) had to get out of bed, walk across the cold floor to the other side of the house and adjust the thermostat.

After several weeks of doing that, I had an idea to make the process a lot easier. I called it "the string thing." I first tied a string to the adjustment lever of the thermostat. Then I ran the string through dozens of eye hooks that had been placed down the hallway, around the door frame, across the bedroom ceiling, and ended up against the wall about two feet above our bed. I tied a washer to the end of the string above our bed. In the morning I just reached up and pulled on the washer, which would move the thermostat lever at the other side of the house, and the floor furnace would ignite with a loud roar. That roar became one of Diana's favorite sounds. She would grab her robe, put on her slippers, run to the furnace and stand on top of it. Her robe would fill up with hot air and a smile would appear on her face.

When we choose the power of the Holy Spirit, it does not mean we do nothing. It means we do what we can do and allow the Spirit of God to do what we cannot do.

The same dynamic happens with us and the Holy Spirit. If we have asked Jesus to live in our heart, then the pilot light of the Spirit's presence is inside us. However, the Spirit is present in us to be more than a pilot light. His desire is to roar into flame and burn away everything inside us that is not of God, and empower us to live the life and vision to which God has called us.

But how does that happen? How does the Holy Spirit's presence change from a pilot light to a roaring presence that consumes and controls us?

First, we have to acknowledge that we want to be consumed and controlled by the Holy Spirit of God. John the Baptist made a statement about his life and the life of Jesus: *"He must become greater; I must become less"* (John 3:30). The same statement will be said by us when we want more of Jesus and less of ourselves.

Second, we have to acknowledge that there are only two sources of power to live life: there is the power of God through the Holy Spirit and then all other powers. We have a choice every moment of every day as to the power supply upon which we will draw. When we choose the power of the Holy Spirit, it does not mean we do nothing. It means we do what we can do and allow the Spirit of God to do what we cannot do. As a result, we partner with the Holy Spirit, are empowered by the Holy Spirit, and live the vision God has given us. On the other hand, we can choose to rely upon power other than the Holy Spirit. If that is our choice, we might accomplish many things—but they will be for our glory, not the glory of Jesus. They will be temporal, not eternal. They will build up our name, not the kingdom of God.

Third, it is important to know that it takes a lifetime to turn our whole life over to Jesus so we can be totally consumed by the power of the Holy Spirit. Jesus was the only One who has, or will ever be totally filled with the Spirit, completely led by the Spirit, and totally consumed by the power of the Spirit (Luke 4:1, 14).

That is not stated to be discouraging. It is stated as reality because our humanness will never allow us to completely rid our life of sin

165

and completely give ourselves to God. There is a way we can choose to live so that in spite of our sinfulness, more and more of our life is empowered by the Holy Spirit and made available for Christ and His kingdom.

As someone once said to me, "The question is not how much of Christ do we have? Rather the question is how much of us does Christ have?" Christ will have more and more of us as we continually increase spiritual disciplines into our lives. Among the spiritual disciplines are:

- prayer
- Bible reading
- meditation
- service
- worship

Life is not supposed to be just about us. It is about us making ourselves available to Christ, being empowered by His Holy spirit, and living and serving to be a blessing to others.

It is Godself who creates us, who forgives and redeems us, and who empowers us to live daily. That is why Godself is a gift we can't afford to lose.

Questions

■ What thoughts come to your mind after reading the bridge story?

- Is there a "bridge" in your life – a place or event or memory or feeling that covers you with fear?

- How can Godself change that?

- How did Godself walk Noah through possible bridges?

- Where do Jesus and the Holy Spirit get involved in your personal story?

12

Gift Twelve

Life

What shall we say, then? Shall we go on sinning so that grace may increase? By no means! We died to sin; how can we live in it any longer? Or don't you know that all of us who were baptized into Christ Jesus were baptized into his death? We were therefore buried with him through baptism into death in order that, just as Christ was raised from the dead through the glory of the Father, we too may live a new life.

For if we have been united with him like this in his death, we will certainly also be united with him in his resurrection. For we know that our old self was crucified with him, so that the body of sin might be done away with, that we should no longer be slaves to sin—because anyone who has died has been freed from sin.

Now if we died with Christ, we believe that we will also live with him. For we know that since Christ was raised from the dead, he cannot die again; death no longer has mastery over him. The death he died, he died to sin once for all; but the life he lives, he lives to God.

In the same way, count yourselves dead to sin but alive to God in Christ Jesus. Therefore do not let sin reign in your mortal body so that you obey its evil desires. Do not offer the parts of your body to sin, as instruments of wickedness, but rather offer yourselves to God, as those who have been brought from death to life; and offer the parts of your body to him as instruments of righteousness.

—Romans 6:1–13

Several years ago I spoke at the funeral of a well-known person in our community. The sadness of the situation was tragically compounded by the fact that this person had committed suicide. Because of the circumstances surrounding his death, I did not have the opportunity to speak directly to the family prior to the service. They did give me a biographical summary and other comments about his life. Other people who knew him spoke about him at the service. My responsibility was to bring a pastoral and Biblical perspective to this tragic situation. I thought and prayed about my words for an entire day. God gave me a few words I still remember. Those few words were: God does not judge a life by how it ends. Rather, we are judged by our decision to either accept or reject Jesus as our personal Lord and Savior.

Does that mean we can just accept Jesus, and then live like we please? No and yes. The answer is no, if living like we please means living like we did before accepting Jesus. The answer is yes, if we agree with Paul in Romans 6 that once we accept Jesus we will not want to live any other way except to please Him.

Paul is emphasizing that after we choose Jesus, we still have another significant choice to make. That choice is: how will we live life? Will we be an instrument of sin or an instrument of righteousness?

Diana and I enjoy swing dancing. We normally dance to music recorded on a CD, but we have also danced to music from a live band. A live band is fantastic. However, what would happen if just one musician played off-key or played the wrong song? It would make the whole band sound bad.

The same dynamic is true in our life. Obviously we cannot be totally free from sin. By relying on the power of the Holy Spirit we can make it our aim to live a righteous and holy life in every area. This means we are going to be the same person everywhere we are—at home, church, work, involved in our hobby, watching our children play sports, or driving our car. We do not always have a choice in what happens to us, but we do have a choice in how we respond to what happens to us.

No matter what, we have a choice in how we live—whether we choose to live as a God-honoring instrument of righteousness or choose to be an instrument of sin and destruction.

This dynamic of choice is very clear in the story of Noah. Noah did not have to choose to live the life he did. Instead of how he was described in Genesis 6:9, he could have chosen to be an unrighteous man, full of blame, and one who did not walk with God. Yet, he chose to be the man he was, day after day, week after week, month after month, and year after year. I encourage us all to live a God-honoring life like Noah because life is a gift we can't afford to lose. There are several important lessons to remember about the gift of life.

First, there is nothing in our past that will keep God from loving us.

In Genesis 5:29, we read about the birth of Noah. Three verses later Noah is five hundred years old. It is not possible for Noah to have lived five hundred years and have no sin. Even Noah was included in the statement about humankind in Genesis 6:5, *"every inclination of the thoughts of his heart was only evil all the time."*

The difference for Noah was that in the midst of his sinfulness he made three wise decisions. First, he relied upon the mercy and grace of God that I believe he learned from the example of his great-grandfather, Enoch. This mercy and grace means that God will not reject us because of our sinfulness but will keep on loving us in the midst of our sinfulness. Second, he did not use his sin as an excuse to separate himself from God. Third, he chose to live as righteous and God-honoring as possible in spite of his sin.

We do not know what Noah's sin was and we do not need to know. From God's perspective, there was nothing in Noah's past that would keep God from loving him. Is there anything in your past that you believe is so big or so horrible that God has chosen not to love you? From your perspective the answer might be yes. From God's perspective the answer is always no. No matter what is in your past, God still loves you.

Second, there is nothing in our present that will stop God from inviting us to be an instrument of His kingdom.

We might not hear His invitation when He gives it, but He is always inviting us to be an instrument of His kingdom. Do we believe that Noah was the only one who was asked by God to build the ark? And in the one hundred years it took to build, do we believe that Noah never asked anyone to help him? It would be very consistent with other parts of the Bible if God only spoke to Noah about the vision. However, it is difficult for me to comprehend that Noah remained silent in offering the invitation for others to help. I am not saying the ark was like Tom Sawyer's fence-painting party. I understand it is more like the disciple Andrew telling his brother, Simon, about Jesus. In John 1:40–42 we read, *"Andrew, Simon Peter's brother, was one of the two who heard what John had said and who had followed Jesus. The first thing Andrew did was to find his brother Simon and tell him, 'We have found the Messiah' (that is, the Christ). And he brought him to Jesus."*

When Noah got the vision from God, I believe one of the first things he did was to act like Andrew and extend the invitation for others to help. Simon responded to Andrew's invitation; that we know. Did Andrew extend the invitation to anyone else? I believe he did, but only God knows how many people responded. Even Jesus extended an invitation to people who did not accept it. The most obvious example is the invitation given to the rich young man, recorded in Mark 10. The reason given for him to decline the invitation of Jesus was *"because he had great wealth"* (Mark 10:22). How many others declined the invitation of Jesus? We will never know.

How many responded to Noah's invitation? We will never know that either, but it is a very common opinion that no one helped Noah except the other seven on the ark.

Why did other people reject Noah's invitation? There are countless possible reasons but the others all had one thing in common: they allowed the noise of sin to be louder than the voice of God.

God is continually extending His invitation for us to be an instrument of His kingdom. The question we each need to ask is this: is the noise of sin louder in my life than the voice of God? If it is, and you want to hear the voice of God more than the noise of sin, it is important to follow these steps:

Confess your sin to Jesus.

Repent of your sin.

Ask Jesus for forgiveness.

Believe in the promise of 1 John 1:9, *"If we confess our sins, He [Jesus] is faithful and just and will forgive us our sins and purify us from all unrighteousness."*

Choose to live a life that honors Jesus in every way.

Practicing these steps on a very frequent basis will begin to quiet the noise of sin. In addition, the Holy Spirit is always working to open up the ears of our heart, so we can hear the voice of God. It is not easy, but it is worth it because of the person you will become and the way God can more fully use you as an instrument in His kingdom.

Third, there is nothing in our future that will cause God to stop holding us in the palm of His hand.

One of the many fascinating parts of the story of Noah is that we do not know any specific details during the last 350 years of his life: *"After the flood Noah lived 350 years. Altogether, Noah lived 950 years, and then he died"* (Genesis 9:28–29). We do not know where he lived, and we do not know what he did. Because of what we read in Genesis 9:20 we can speculate that he was a farmer for the rest of his life: *"Noah, a man of the soil, proceeded to plant a vineyard."* So maybe Noah farmed the land, lived with his wife, and the two of them grew old together. That would be a nice ending, but what happened between Noah and God in Noah's last 350 years? Did he walk out of the ark and say, "I'm glad that is over," and then never talk to God again? Did God never use Noah for any other task? Did He ever give him any other vision?

We cannot answer these questions about Noah. However, I believe that there is nothing in our future that will stop God from holding us in the palm of His hand: *"Where can I go from your Spirit? Where can I flee from your presence? If I go up to the heavens, you are there; if I make my bed in the depths, you are there. If I rise on the wings of the dawn, if I settle on the far side of the sea, even there your hand will guide me, your right hand will hold me fast"* (Psalm 139:7–10).

From this Psalm we learn a very important characteristic of God. He will never let us go. There is nothing in our future that will cause God to stop holding us in the palm of His hand.

If we choose to spend eternity with Him, He will be holding us. If we choose to reject Him and spend eternity in hell, He will still be holding us even though we will not recognize it, acknowledge it, or know it. How can God, who is everywhere, not also be present in hell? Is God's love and grasp so weak that He would let go of people who have rejected Him for all eternity? I think not.

For Noah, I believe he chose to continue living a righteous life, always available to God for friendship, conversation, or a new vision.

What about you? Your future has not yet been written. You can choose to live it any way you want—as an instrument of God or as an instrument of sin. Either way, there is nothing that will happen in your future that will cause God to stop holding you in the palm of His hand.

The question is this: when you pass from this life to life eternal, will you do so acknowledging God's hand around you, or will you be in darkness and completely unaware of it?

Eternity is too long to be wrong. Life on earth and eternal life with God are both the gifts we can't afford to lose.

Questions

- What are your feelings about this comment: "There is nothing in our past that will keep God from loving us"?

- Why do we often struggle to grasp that truth?

- Do you believe: "There is nothing in our present that will stop God from inviting us to be an instrument of His kingdom"?

- Write a list of what you've learned through this book to help make that statement a reality in your life.

- How can Noah's story help you believe this: "There is nothing in our future that will cause God to stop holding us in the palm of His hand"?

IF YOU'RE A FAN OF THIS BOOK, PLEASE TELL OTHERS

- Write a positive review on www.amazon.com.

- Purchase additional copies to give away as gifts.

- Suggest *12 Gifts We Can't Afford to Lose* to friends.

- Write about *12 Gifts We Can't Afford to Lose* on your blog. Post excerpts to your social media sites such as: Facebook, Twitter, Pinterest, Instagram, etc.

- When you're in a bookstore, ask if they carry the book. The book is available through all major distributors, so any bookstore that does not have it in stock can easily order it.

You can order additional copies of the book from my website as well as in bookstores by going to **www.trinityarl.com**. Special bulk quantity discounts are available.

Trinity Sports Ministry

Of all the ways to spread the Gospel message, sports might
be the last way you would consider. And yet, sports—
or more specifically, a sports ministry—is a simple, yet
powerful way to engage children, youth and families with
the message of the Gospel.

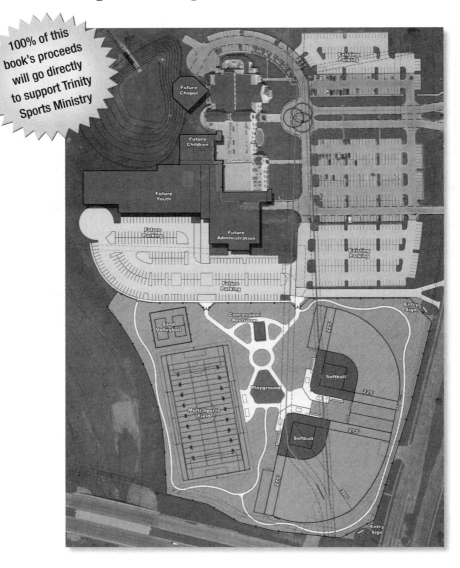

100% of this book's proceeds will go directly to support Trinity Sports Ministry

"Go Therefore and Make Disciples of All Nations"

In order to help fulfill the above words of Jesus, Trinity Sports Ministry (TSM) plans to introduce and foster a love of Jesus Christ to un-churched and under-churched children, youth and families by developing a Christian sports ministry in Arlington, Texas. This sports ministry will provide the community and surrounding areas with a safe, fun and Christian-based environment in which to play and learn.

In addition to the activity center/gymnasium that has already been built, a future multi-sport athletic complex will include a variety of outdoor fields for sports teams of all ages. The goal of TSM is not merely to entertain, but to provide children, youth and families with a positive, life-changing encounter through Christian adults who will be available as coaches, mentors and friends.

All of the proceeds from the sale of *12 Gifts We Can't Afford To Lose* will go directly to support Trinity Sports Ministry.

If you want to make a positive Christian impact in the lives of children and youth, then consider becoming a TSM Booster. You can pray, volunteer, give financially, or sponsor a child, youth, or an entire team to help this vision become a reality.

For more information, see our website at: **trinitysportsministry.com.**

Ready for More Gifts?

Hopefully reading this book has awakened a fresh awareness of the faithfulness of God in your life. A great way to more fully "unwrap" these 12 gifts is through personal devotion and discussion with others.

12 Gifts We Can't Afford to Lose
— Small Group Study —

This 12-session interactive study includes video presentations, daily personal devotions, and engaging discussion questions, all designed to help you more fully embrace these 12 gifts of God's faithfulness.